Narrative Analysis

Social Research and Educational Studies Series

Series Editor
Robert G. Burgess,
Professor of Sociology,
University of Warwick

Narrative Analysis

Martin Cortazzi

22 The Falmer Press

(A member of the Taylor & Francis Group)
London • Washington, D.C.

UK   The Falmer Press, 4 John Street, London WC1N 2ET
USA   The Falmer Press, Taylor & Francis Inc., 1900 Frost Road, Suite 101, Bristol, PA 19007

First published in 1993

A catalogue record for this book is available from the British Library

Library of Congress Cataloging-in-Publication Data are available on request

ISBN 1 85000 9627 (cased)
ISBN 1 85000 9635 (paper)

Jacket design by Caroline Archer

Typeset in 11/13pt Garamond by
Graphicraft Typesetters Ltd., Hong Kong.

Printed in Great Britain by Burgess Science Press, Basingstoke on paper which has a specified pH value on final paper manufacture of not less than 7.5 and is therefore 'acid free'.

Contents

Contents

Series Editor's Preface

The purpose of the Social Research and Educational Studies Series is to provide authoritative guides to key issues in educational research. The series includes overviews of field, guidance on good practice and discussions of the practical implications of social and educational research. In particular, the series details with a variety of approaches to conducting social and educational research. Contributors to this series review recent work, raise critical concerns that are particular to the field of education, and reflect on the implications of research for educational policy and practice.

Each volume in the series draws on material that will be relevant for an international audience. The contributors to this series all have wide experience of teaching, conducting and using educational research. The volumes are written so that they will appeal to a wide audience of students, teachers and researchers. Altogether, the volumes in the Social Research and Educational Studies Series provide a comprehensive guide for anyone concerned with contemporary educational research.

The series will include individually authored books and edited volumes on a range of themes in education including qualitative research, survey research, the interpretation of data, self-evaluation, research and social policy, analyzing data, action research and the politics and ethics of research.

Many of the volumes on social research that are currently available deal with standard topics. However, Martin Cortazzi's book on Narrative Analysis provides a systematic introduction to a field that seldom gets detailed treatment in the scope of one text. He demonstrates the use of a variety of different models of narrative analysis in relation to the study of educational settings. This book provides many useful examples that will stimulate researchers, teachers and students to engage in narrative analysis in the conduct of social and educational research.

Robert Burgess
Series Editor

Acknowledgments

I should like to thank Maurice Galton and Sara Delamont for encouraging my research into narrative, Robert Burgess for his support as series editor, and Diana Cortazzi for reading through draft chapters. Many thanks also to Roy Kirk and his staff at the library in the School of Education at the University of Leicester for helping me to get hold of many books and articles. Finally, warm thanks to the teachers whose narratives form the data analyzed in chapter 6: they gave up their time to be interviewed and I am grateful to them.

Chapter 1

Introduction

Teachers' thoughts, perceptions, beliefs and experience are all aspects of teachers' culture which we need to know about and be aware of as a key factor in education, especially in times of change. Yet this crucial aspect of education is probably undervalued and certainly underresearched. Educational investigations, in general, have paid too little attention to teachers' voices. Teachers' culture is largely unexamined, except by ethnographic studies and case studies, which necessarily deal with small numbers. An increasing number of scholars are suggesting, however, that narrative research offers a way for us to hear teachers' voices and begin to understand their culture from the inside.

This book examines a variety of approaches to narrative and shows that narrative analysis can allow us to study teachers' culture and thinking, both qualitatively and quantitatively. Use of narrative methods of research can allow us to develop descriptions of teachers' culture which preserve their voices.

The fundamental importance of narrative can be gathered from some of the epithets used to describe it. Narrative is 'a primary act of mind' (Hardy, 1987, p. 1), 'the primary scheme by means of which human existence is rendered meaningful' (Polkinghorne, 1988, p. 11), 'a means by which human beings represent and restructure the world' (Mitchell, 1981, p. 8). It is 'a specific cultural system' (Fawcett *et al.*, 1984, p. 20), the 'organizing principle' by which 'people organize their experience in, knowledge about, and transactions with the social world' (Bruner, 1990, p. 35). When people tell stories, anecdotes and other kinds of narratives they are engaged in 'a perceptual activity that organizes data into a special pattern which represents and explains experience' (Branigan, 1992, p. 3). By studying oral accounts of personal experience we can examine the tellers' representations and explanations of experience. Thus Chafe (1990) sees narratives 'as overt manifestations of the mind in action: as windows to both the content of the mind and its ongoing operations.' (p. 79). Narrative analysis can, therefore, be seen as opening a window on the mind, or, if we are analyzing narratives of a specific group of tellers, as opening a window on their culture. With this recognition of the importance of narrative as a major semiotic mode it is perhaps not surprising that some scholars have come to regard 'narratology' as an independent discipline studying the theory of narrative texts (Todorov, 1969; Prince, 1982; Bal, 1985; Chatman, 1988). More usually, researchers have regarded narrative as a field on which a number of disciplines, each with its own focus, converge.

In this way Toolan (1988) treats narrative from the perspectives of literary theory and sociolinguistics, Hendricks (1973) views it in terms of folklore and linguistics, while van Dijk (1984) analyzes narratives by combining psychological and sociolinguistic models. Brewer (1985) explores the implications of narrative research for education by linking psychological with anthropological findings, while Coles (1989) does so by examining narrative in psychiatry and literature. By weaving psychological and literary themes, Bruner (1986 and 1990) presents sharp insights into narrative, which are widely quoted in educational contexts. Polkinghorne (1988) examines narrative in history, literature, psychology and philosophy to seek insights for practitioners who work with narrative knowledge in the form of case histories and narrative explanations.

Some scholars cross the disciplinary boundaries by working with others in another discipline. Thus de Beaugrande and Colby (1979) bring together linguistics and anthropology in their work on narrative, Labov and Fanshel (1977) collaborate from linguistic and psychotherapeutic backgrounds and Kintsch and van Dijk (1983) bring their linguistic and cognitive psychology expertise to bear on narrative study. Contributors to Sarbin's volume (1986) and Britton's and Pellegrini's collection of papers (1990) move from starting points in psychology to range over issues in psychiatry, child development, literacy, discourse and the history of science.

Given such numerous multidisciplinary efforts at narrative research over two decades it seems unwise, and wasteful, for those engaged in narrative study in education to ignore work done in other disciplines. Yet most of the current surge of published work on narrative in education makes little reference to disciplines outside education. The potential for educational researchers to use the knowledge, draw on the insights and apply the models and findings already obtained and developed elsewhere is enormous. To realize at least part of this potential we need to have some familiarity with work on narrative done in other disciplines.

Chapter 2 of this book surveys some of the current approaches to narrative and the study of teaching. Some methods of using narrative among teachers are examined, including personal journals, personal histories, collaborative biographies, autobiographies, and methods using narrative inquiry and curriculum stories. To broaden the base for considering narrative analysis in education the following chapters each draw on work from different disciplines.

In chapter 3 sociological and sociolinguistic models of narrative are examined. The chapter draws attention to ways in which stories arise in interaction and are often in effect jointly produced by several people. It shows how the internal structure of narratives can be analyzed and related to the social context of the telling, specifically the context of research interviews.

Chapter 4 outlines psychological approaches to narrative by focussing on the processes of understanding, recalling and summarizing stories. The constructive nature of memory is emphasized, whether people tell stories they have read in experimental situations or whether they remember real life events in natural contexts.

Some concepts of narrative from literary study are delineated in chapter 5. While literary theory has focussed primarily on novels and short stories, a number of scholars have paid detailed attention to oral stories in order to understand basic problems of narrative: how to define and describe the major characteristics of narrative.

In chapter 6 anthropological models of narrative are examined. The chapter shows how the structure, function and performance of stories may vary cross-culturally. Different cultural groups have different ways of speaking and hold different ideas about narrative.

Each of these chapters looks for implications and applications from within different disciplines for the use of methods of narrative analysis within education. A question throughout is: how might we apply insights, methods and techniques of narrative analysis to the study of teachers' narratives? Any answers are, of course, fairly likely to be applicable to using narrative analysis as a research tool with other occupational groups or throughout the social sciences.

Chapter 7 shows an application of narrative research by reporting a detailed analysis of 123 British primary teachers' narratives. The narratives were collected in both research interviews and natural situations. They were analyzed in different categories: teachers' stories about children, classroom learning, humorous events and classroom disasters, and trouble with parents. Common features are found showing a broad cultural picture of the perspectives and experiences of the teachers. Several levels of narrative analysis are reported, demonstrating that narrative analysis can be used effectively as an innovative technique in educational research.

Chapter 2

Narrative and the Study of Teaching

The study of teachers' narratives — teachers' stories of their own experiences — is increasingly being seen as central to the study of teachers' thinking, culture and behaviour. There are those who argue that it is crucial to understand these aspects of teachers' lives if current efforts at improvements and reforms of a number of educational systems around the world are to be effective. Any real change in the curriculum is not likely to be carried through unless teachers' perceptions and experiences are taken into account. Among these advocates is Louden (1991): 'The teacher is the ultimate key to educational change and school improvement . . . Teachers don't merely deliver the curriculum. They develop it, define it and reinterpret it too. It is what teachers think, what teachers believe and what teachers do at the level of the classroom that ultimately shapes the kind of learning that young people get' (p. vi).

To improve educational systems, curriculum reforms and classroom practice, therefore, we need to know more about teachers' perspectives. We need to know how teachers themselves see their situation, what their experience is like, what they believe and how they think. In short, we need to know more about teachers' culture, from the inside. This is an important area of education which until recently has received little attention from researchers.

This book proposes that the analysis of teachers' narratives can be used as an innovative methodology to study such questions of teachers' culture, experience and beliefs. To appreciate this methodology it is necessary to understand the importance of teachers' narratives. Then it is vital to know something about how narratives work, socially and psychologically, and to see how narratives are structured. With this kind of foundation, we shall be in a strong position to examine methods of narrative analysis and apply them to current research concerns about teaching.

This chapter takes up the first of these points, looking at some of the reasons why teachers' narratives have become prominent among the concerns of many researchers and seeing how narrative analysis is currently being developed in education. Later chapters will look for further knowledge and insights about narrative by surveying approaches to narrative from a number of social science disciplines. A detailed application of narrative research to teachers' narratives is given in the final chapter which focusses on the author's study of nearly 1000 British primary teachers' narratives.

Three current trends of research about teachers point to the importance of teachers' narratives. These trends are centred around the concepts of 'reflection', the nature of teachers' knowledge, and 'voice'.

Reflection

Reflection is a concept which has been much discussed in teacher education of late. There are, however, different views of what the term means. Schwab (1971) argued that it is theory applied to action; 'deliberation' involves problem-solving by drawing on the greatest number of genuinely pertinent concerns. More influential has been Schon's (1983 and 1987) concept of 'reflection on action' where theory emerges from the knowledge base generated from action or earlier experience. Others have sought to develop the implications of 'reflective teaching' (Zeichner and Liston, 1987; Pollard and Tann, 1987; Tabachnik and Zeichner, 1991) or of 'reflective learning' (Boyd and Fales, 1983) and 'reflective practice' (Sergiovanni, 1985) for training teachers. These notions are often traced back to Dewey's (1938b) notion of reflective action, where teachers are encouraged to act with intent by reflecting systematically on their experience. Indeed, Dewey (1910 and 1938a) defined thinking and logic as the reflective reconstruction of experience, a phrase which also neatly describes narrative.

Of the various strategies currently being used to encourage reflection, two stand out as having a narrative nature: keeping personal journals or logs and writing personal histories and autobiographies. Both of these strategies essentially ask teachers to narrate their experience as a way of reflecting on it and learning from it.

Personal journals are advocated as a means of promoting reflective teaching by forcing the writers to learn about what they know, what they feel, what they do (and how they do it) and why they do it (Yinger and Clark, 1981 quoted in Maas, 1991, p. 215). The writing of a journal is 'both constructing experience and reconstructing it' (Holly, 1989, p. 76). Guided by a tutor or supervisor, this enables the writer — as a student teacher or an experienced teacher — to view experiences in broader educational contexts. Journal writers become aware not only of their perspectives on children, classrooms and learning but also to 'learn about the lenses through which they are viewing children and teaching' (*ibid*, p. 75). As Grumet (1990) puts it, 'To reread the journal is to see oneself seeing' (p. 321). Thus the process of reading and rereading the journal after some interval of time should, it is hoped, bring awareness of the writer's perspectives on education, the ability to notice what children are learning etc. and to become aware of how these things are themselves developing.

In this vein, Maas (1991) gets small groups of students to tell stories about their teaching, from memory or from notes in journals. These are collected, discussed and redirected back to the students through a newsletter. They become part of a dialogue with peers and supervisor. The supervisor also responds to stories written in journals. This interaction of reflection, telling and audience reaction may be more significant in fostering reflection, Maas suggests, than the cognitive benefits of writing alone.

Similarly, White (1991) gets students to tell 'war stories', and to listen to those of an experienced teacher, in order to encourage them to reflect on their practice as a means of becoming aware of their central premises about teaching.

Connelly and Clandinin (1988, pp. 44–8) use storytelling as a tool for teachers to reflect on personal practical knowledge. They ask teachers to write three detailed, shareable stories of themselves in the classroom. These are then shared in pairs with teachers they trust, to ask how the stories express a view of learners, subject content, teaching, classroom relationships and the educational context. Finally larger collections of stories are examined to search for patterns.

Richert (1991) uses 'case methods' — descriptions of actual teaching situations — in the same way: 'studying cases actually relies on a dialectic between events and meanings, practice and theory. We learn from the narrative as we reflect on the content and make sense if it based on what we know and believe . . . cases are stories that help us learn about classroom life' (pp. 140–1). All these approaches are essentially using narrative accounts to teach teacher reflection.

The benefits of writing a personal journal depend on the honesty and sincerity of the writer and on the sensitivity and responsiveness of the reader or supervisor. To some extent they depend on whether, and how, the writer re-reads what has been written and reads and responds to a supervisor's or peers' comments. This implies that both parties are working within an interactive model of training or teacher development, where learning takes place in interaction between participants. It is often the case, however, that students and teachers approach education courses with a transmission model in mind, expecting the supervisor or lecturer to explain or demonstrate methodology or subject content. Journal writing seems much more interactive than this. The sequence may be: classroom activity — reflection and writing — someone's response to the writing — joint construction of interpretation — next classroom activity.

Personal histories — accounts of first-hand experiences of learning and of being in a school — are 'an important and powerful dimension in our pedagogical thinking' (Knowles and Holt-Reynolds, 1991, p. 87). This strategy of asking students to write personal histories of education assists new teachers to become aware of their own belief system, 'an initial perspective against which they can begin to make personal choices about how they will behave as teachers' (*ibid*). It draws on students' many years of observing and participating in classrooms, as pupils, and attempts to make key aspects of teaching explicit through narrative.

Louden (1991, p. 149) worked alongside a classroom teacher in an effort to understand how teachers' knowledge changes over time. He noted how teachers' personal reflection in personal history and story is aimed at achieving a deeper, clearer understanding of the teaching situation. It typically involves replay and rehearsal of professional action, the review of classroom events through stories. The role of narrative is clear in his comment: 'Because our teaching was such a stream of unreflective experience I've needed to replay these stories in order to make meaning of the experiences we shared. These stories may not be very technical . . . but they were stories which needed to be told if the experience were to contribute to our development as teachers' (p. 172).

In this view, the act of narrating one's experience as a teacher focusses reflection on key classroom events and helps the teller of the story to make sense of what has happened. The experience is relived in the context of relevant questions: How did this happen? What was the cause of that? What might have happened if . . .? It is reenacted in response to audience comments. Thus at its best reflection through narrative effectively doubles the value of the original experience — an efficient approach to teacher development.

Teachers' Knowledge

The nature of teachers' knowledge has also been linked to teachers' narratives. Explorations of what teachers know, how they think and learn professionally or make decisions in the classroom is a clearly developing major strand of research about teaching (Calderhead, 1987 and 1988). Perhaps surprisingly, we do not know much about what teachers know. Even more importantly, we do not know much about how they come to learn. Yet what teachers know and learn is clearly crucial to our understanding of educational processes and how children may be taught.

Teachers' classroom knowledge can be thought of as 'high context knowledge' in the sense that most of the relevant information necessary to interpret what teachers say is either in the physical context or internalized in the person. Relatively little of it needs to be expressed explicitly or communicated as such in the classroom so it is not readily articulated by the teacher (Elbaz, 1990, p. 21). This is in contrast to the 'low context' knowledge developed by educational researchers, which is more explicit and less tied to any particular context.

Teachers' knowledge has also been characterized as 'personal practical knowledge' (Connelly and Clandinin, 1988). This is not academic knowledge, but is built from personal and professional experience. This description is intended to indicate how teachers' knowledge seems to be a particular way of reconstructing the past, combined with intention for the future to deal with the needs of present situations. Similarly, Doyle (1990) has noted how teachers' knowledge is 'event structured': 'What teachers know about chunks of context, instructional actions, or management strategies is tied to specific events they have experienced in classrooms . . . Teachers' knowledge is fundamentally particularistic and situational. Their knowledge is, in other words, case knowledge.' (pp. 355–6).

This event-structured knowledge, where reconstructions of past situations and cases play a major role, is inevitably frequently expressed in narrative. Teachers' descriptions take on a narrative character. As Feiman-Nemser and Floden (1985) put it: 'Caught up in the demands of their own work, teachers cannot solve problems in general; they must deal with specific situations. Thus their descriptions of teaching sound more like stories than theories because they are full of the particulars of their own experience' (p. 513).

Elbaz (1990, p. 30), in tracing the evolution of research on teachers' thinking, notes 'the sheer presence of story' within the research work and comes to the conclusion that story 'is beginning to acquire a sort of pedigree in the form of a complex theoretical backdrop for our discussion . . . "story" is that which most adequately constitutes and presents teachers' knowledge . . . story is the very stuff of teaching, the landscape within which we live as teachers and researchers' (*ibid*, pp. 31–2).

In exploring the nature of teachers' knowledge, then, we need to take account of how much of it is expressed in stories — for good reasons, given the context-bound nature of classroom experience and the event-structured nature of teachers' knowledge. Teachers' narratives express their knowledge of classroom practice and some of this knowledge could not, we can conclude, be expressed in any other way. All of this suggests that studying teachers' stories could be a productive way of finding out more about teachers' knowledge.

Teachers' Voices

The current concern with teachers' 'voices' has also been firmly linked to narrative. 'Voice' is a term increasingly used by those concerned with teacher empowerment (Goodson, 1991 and 1992). The term emphasizes the need for teachers to talk about their experiences and perspectives on teaching in their own words as part of the current debate and process of change in education which affects, among others, the teachers themselves. Proponents of teachers' voice argue that teachers are key participants in education, that they should be heard and that they have a right to speak for and about teaching.

The absence of teachers' voices has been noted by several observers: 'In the world of teacher development the central ingredient so far missing is the teacher's voice. Primarily the concern has been on the teacher's practice' (Goodson, 1991, p. 141). 'Conspicuous by their absence from the literature of research on teaching are the voices of the teachers themselves — the questions and problems that teachers pose, the frameworks they use to interpret and improve their practice, and the ways teachers themselves define and understand their work lives' (Lytle and Cochran-Smith, 1990, p. 83).

There is, therefore, increasing recognition that it is fundamental to our understanding of teaching that it should be known by others as teachers know it. Thus Butt and his colleagues work as researchers alongside teachers using the teachers' narrative accounts so that, as outsiders, they can approach classroom reality in terms of the teacher's voice. The biographer and teacher work collaboratively to provide 'a vehicle for recording and interpreting the *teacher's voice*'. They do so in several senses. 'In a physical and metaphorical sense, the tone, the quality, the feelings that are conveyed by the way a teacher speaks are important to consider in interpreting the nature of teaching. In a political sense, the teacher's voice attests to the *right* of speaking and being represented . . . "Voice" also connotes that what is said is *characteristic*

Table 1:   *Grumet's Model of Voices in Educational Theory*

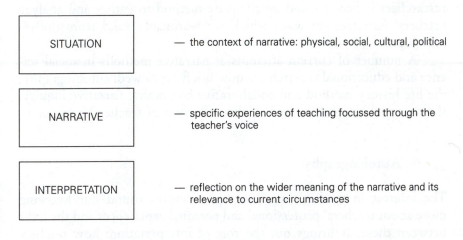

of teachers, as distinct from other potential voices' (Butt and Raymond, 1987, p. 76).

The narrative account must therefore carry the teacher's voice if researchers and other observers are to know what a teacher knows or feels. Indeed, how can anyone else know what is inside the teacher's head or heart without the teacher's commentary?

The teacher's voice may emerge at its strongest in teachers' narrative accounts. Grumet (1990) gives narrative a major role in her proposal of a triad for the voices of educational theory. 'Let our songs have three parts, situation, narrative and interpretation. The first, situation, acknowledges that we tell our story as a speech act that involves the social, cultural and political relations in and to which we speak. Narrative ... invites all the specificity, presence and power that the symbolic and semiotic registers of our speaking can provide. And interpretation provides another voice, a reflexive and more distant one' (p. 281). This might be expressed in a diagram as shown in table 1. In effect, a study of teachers' narratives is also potentially a study of their own interpretations of their situation, i.e. their teaching theories.

Elbaz (1990) lists six reasons why story is particularly fitting to make public the teacher's voice (p. 32): story relies on tacit knowledge to be understood; it takes place in a meaningful context; it calls on storytelling traditions which give a structure to expression; it often involves a moral lesson to be learned; it can voice criticism in socially acceptable ways; it reflects the inseparability of thought and action in storytelling performance — the dialogue between teller and audience. Teachers' knowledge is ordered by narrative and is best voiced through teachers telling their own story in their own way. The problem for researchers is how to find an adequate method to gather and analyze teachers' narratives in ways which are reasonably valid from the research point of view.

A number of current attempts at narrative methods in social science and educational research are now briefly reviewed: autobiography, the life history method and collaborative biography, narrative inquiry, the study of curriculum stories, the collection of teachers' anecdotes.

Autobiography

The interest in teacher's autobiography centres round our knowing more about teachers' professional and personal experiences and the links between these. It brings out the role of interpretation: how teachers understand their past work and their past selves. It points to the importance of teachers' self-understanding as a vehicle for personal emancipation and professional development. Self-narrative, it is held, leads to personal and professional transformation.

In this context autobiography has been defined as 'a reconstruction that involves a conscious and reflexive elaboration of much of the author's life, including personal and professional experiences. It provides an interpretation of the episodes of a life and the relation the author has to them' (Diamond, 1991, p. 93).

In this way, Pinar and Grumet (1976) have developed a 'reconceptualist' method, where the curriculum is seen as 'the collective story we tell our children about our past, our present and our future' (Grumet, 1981, p. 115). This curriculum is reconceptualized through critical reflection upon educational experiences. Narrative is a strategy to disclose educational experiences. Autobiography, as self-narrative, becomes a method of reflecting on the self in lived experience. Autobiography is an inquiry into the 'architecture of the self' (Pinar, 1988), which shows the author how experience has been construed and reveals ways in which the curriculum has helped to grind the perceptual lens of the writer.

The key question behind this approach is: What has been and what is the nature of any educational experience? Pinar and Grumet (1976) approach this in four steps. First, regression, teachers are encouraged to turn to the past, focussing on educational experiences. They record them, including their present responses to those experiences. Second, progression, writers look to their future to discuss where their intellectual interests and career might be going. Third, analysis, they describe their biographic present, excluding the past and future but including their responses to these. In a fourth step, synthesis, the teachers put all three pictures together.

This is not just a matter of writing down one's educational experiences, though this is part of the process. Rather, the benefit consists in the critical reflection on those experiences to understand what principles and patterns have been at work in one's educational life. Experiences are reclaimed through reflection. The act of producing a narrative text transforms and externalizes the experience giving writers the opportunity to distance themselves from the experience in order to analyze it. The aim is that teachers, as writers of their selves, should become active interpreters of their past, so that this can be transferred to a usable present by writers who can see themselves as responsible for the shape and texture of their own experiences (Grumet, 1980, p. 157). Autobiography is a 'metaphoric bridge . . . built from subjective self-consciousness to objective reality' (Olney, 1972, p. 36). Describing one's own developmental process is also a way of generating it.

Autobiography can therefore be thought of as reflection upon reflection. As part of the recent developments in teacher reflectiveness in education autobiography could have a key narrative role. But current views of autobiography reveal it to be a complex affair: 'There is something curious about autobiography. It is an account given by a narrator in the here and now about a protagonist bearing his name who existed in the there and then, the story terminating in the present when the protagonist fuses with the narrator' (Bruner, 1990, p. 121). This is a notion of multiple voices: the self then, the self now recalling then, the self now interpreting the self then from the present self's perspective, the self now thinking of possible future selves, a possible future self looking back to now to the present self seeing it as if in the past . . . In all of this the role of interpretation is crucial.

To ask pre-service teachers, or even experienced teachers, to engage in autobiography to these degrees of sophistication unaided is perhaps to impose too heavy or too unrealistic a demand. In fact, Grumet and Pinar see the education tutor as having the role of being a hermeneutic helper, 'negotiating the work of reading and interpreting the narratives with their writers' (Grumet, 1990, p. 323). This suggests a heavy investment in one-to-one contact time between tutor and writer. Grumet (1981) also asks students or teachers to read their narratives aloud in a group, so that the group may respond with questions or comments (p. 128). Teachers clearly benefit from analyzing another's experience after they have critically reflected on their own (Grumet, 1980).

In either case, where the original author, the original audience and the contemporary reader were one and the same person the audience has, in fact, been widened. This is inevitable where autobiography is being used in an education course or for research. It becomes clear that the perceived benefits of developing an autobiographic approach will generally only come about with collaboration between the writer and other people. This joint construction of educational lives is taken up explicitly in the collaborative biographic approach.

Collaborative Biographies

Biography in education has been defined as 'a disciplined way of interpreting a person's thought and action in the light of his or her past', 'the formative history of the individual's life experience' (Berk, 1980, p. 94). Berk emphasizes how biography, as narrative structure, includes selection of incidents from a life, arranged and linked with respect to an outcome so that readers can make sense of the individual's experience and understand how that outcome came to pass. Biography thus conceived is a critical procedure of interpreting evidence, rather than merely transcribing data. In education, the aim is to make sense of teachers' thoughts, actions, experience and attitudes by studying the formation of their professional consciousness through their experience.

Collaborative biography is the joint description and interpretation of a teacher's life experience carried out by the teacher concerned working with one or more researchers. This collaboration facilitates a shift from life stories to life histories (Goodson, 1992). A life story is the personal reconstruction of the experience of the teacher, the story told of his/her professional life. A life history draws on a wider range of evidence: interviews discussions, relevant texts and contexts. In this shift from simple narrative to interpretation the life story is located in a broad contextual background which is built up through the joint activity of the teacher and researcher.

There are several levels of narration: the life as lived then; the life as experienced, interpreted to the teacher's self then and now; the life as told to the researcher, presented to a particular audience in a social context for a particular purpose; the life history, as finally agreed by teacher and researcher in a present interpretation of the evidence.

The collaborative biography approach gives the teacher a more extended role than that of sharing an autobiography. The teacher has different voices. The teacher is less a teller of stories and becomes a more equal investigator, actively involved in constructing and clarifying the narrative text over perhaps between three to ten meetings of up to ninety minutes each (Woods, 1985).

The collaborative biographers aim to produce teacher-centred professional knowledge which 'identifies the nature, sources and manner of evolution of that special kind of thinking, action and knowledge that pertains to . . . teaching' (Butt *et al.*, 1992, p. 51).

In attempting such an account of the biographic formation of teacher's knowledge, the researchers take teachers through four stages which can be identified by questions which teachers ask themselves (*ibid*, pp. 62–3). The first question, 'What is the nature of my working reality?', asks teachers to depict their current working environment. The second question, 'How do I think and act in that context?', asks teachers to describe their current pedagogy and curriculum in use. The third, 'How, through my worklife and personal history, did I come to be that way?' encourages teachers to record reflections on their personal and professional lives, related to their present professional thought and action. The fourth, 'How do I wish to become in my professional future?' asks them to project their narrative forwards to the future.

Both Butt *et al.* (1992) and Woods (1985) see teacher validation as being crucial. The teacher tells his/her story. Then the researcher summarizes it and visits the classroom as a participant observer. The researcher then gives the draft account to the teacher for comment and validation. In this way it is claimed that the teacher 'initiates and controls the interpretive activity with the researcher as facilitator' (Butt and Raymond, 1989, p. 407).

The centrality of narrative to education, in the view of collaborative biographers, can be seen in the statement: 'Education exists, in one sense, for the individual and collective life histories of future generations — to give them a sense of personal and social agency in engaging the reality of our current and future world' (Butt *et al.*, 1990, p. 255). If this is true it must be true of learners too, but the collaborative biography approach emphasizes the need to understand the personal and professional formation of the teacher. As Goodson (1992) says, 'In understanding something so intensely personal as teaching it is critical we know about the person the teacher is' (p. 4).

The importance of teachers' biographies is heavily underlined by the growing realization that teachers' classroom practice is partially shaped by their own school experience, as pupils. Teachers may teach as they themselves were taught. A teacher's professional socialization begins when the teacher is a child through many years of watching teachers at work (Acker, 1987, p. 89; Goodson, 1992, p. 13) and this becomes a major element in the teacher's mental schema of teaching, which includes the influential image of self as a teacher. This in turn may become an interpretive filter for the later experiences of pre-service training and early teaching (Knowles, 1992, p. 137). For younger entrants to teacher training, this implicit early apprenticeship may actually be more influential than their professional courses in the formation of pedagogical constructs; for older entrants prior work and other life experiences may equally outweigh training experiences (Powell, 1992).

To explore this important influence of prior experience, techniques of narrative research, such as collaborative biography, are being developed. The use of biography in teacher training and professional development is advocated to raise intending or experienced teachers' awareness of the nature of the influence of their biography or key professional experiences on their professional activity (Woods, 1985; Wood, 1992). Given a variety of fundamental changes in educational practice in recent years this awareness is clearly important to avoid mismatches between ways in which teachers were taught and ways in which they might be expected to teach now. Advocates of autobiography or collaborative autobiography would probably claim that narrative reflection not only develops awareness of a past and its effect on the present but also enables those who engage in it to transcend the past to take charge of their professional destiny untrammelled by a legacy of inappropriate images of teaching.

Proponents of both autobiography and collaborative biography have had to face criticisms. Grumet (1981) admits that the autobiographic method 'bears the stigma of narcissism and privatisation', but asserts that in an evolving method such 'illusions ... need to be exposed and corrected' (p. 116). Butt *et al.* (1992) claim that collaborative biography has been designed with such concerns in mind, that it should not be seen as 'narcissistic and solipsistic, lacking the contrasting "counter-subjective" view of others' (p. 91).

Both groups of researchers are aware of the need to move from understanding individual teachers' lives to understanding teachers collectively, but since both methods are time-consuming there may be an inherent limitation on the numbers of teachers able to be involved with any one researcher at a time. Samples may remain small.

Narrative Inquiry

Other work on teachers' narratives which involves collaboration between a researcher and teacher has been called 'narrative inquiry' (Connolly and Clandinin, 1990). This method differs from collaborative biography because it has less emphasis on method and the life history of the teacher. It focusses less on problematic situations, life transitions and turning points and more on the everyday business of the classroom.

Connelly and Clandinin (1986), unlike Butts *et al.*, start with observed practical events in the classroom. The observer makes field notes, reflecting in action, and then there is an open-ended interview with the teacher, where both reflect on the action, querying the observed practice. A narrative account of the classroom practice is drawn up by the researcher and is validated by the teacher to yield an interpretive reconstruction of curriculum meaning, based on the story of the teacher's personal experience. The observed and the reflected upon are embedded in a 'narrative unity': 'a continuum within a person's experience which renders life experience meaningful through the unity they achieve for the person' (Connelly and Clandinin, 1987, p. 130). This study of narrative is aimed at explicating experiential understanding of teacher thinking in terms of everyday meaning, developing a theory in terms of practice.

Connelly and Clandinin's definition of narrative is somewhat wider than that of others working in this field: 'Narrative refers to the making of meaning through personal experience by way of a process of reflection in which storytelling is a key element and in which metaphors and folk knowledge take their place' (1988a, p. 16). They see metaphors and images from stories of experience as having an influence on a teacher's future teaching, 'Situations call forth our images from our narratives of experience, and these images are available to act as guides to future action' (1988b, p. 60). Raising teachers' awareness of their images is one way in which narrative inquiry can enable teachers to rethink the curriculum and their teaching. These narrative images influence the personal curriculum of the teacher and this crucial point will be discussed further in chapter 6.

Teachers' Curriculum Stories

The use of curriculum stories by teachers in the classroom has been investigated by Egan (1988 and 1989) and Gudmundsdottir (1990 and 1991). Egan proposes that teachers should use canonical story elements in curriculum planning in order to harness the imaginative and affective elements of narrative for children's learning. Gudmundsdottir investigates experienced teachers' behaviour and thinking in planning and teaching curriculum areas through the use of stores. Both see narratives as potentially organizing the entire curriculum. This notion goes considerably beyond other contemporary developments where story-tellers are advocating that teachers should tell — not read — stories in their classrooms, and encourage their pupils to do so, as a major means to develop important skills of oral language in the English subject area of the curriculum (Rosen, 1988 and 1991) or as part of a programme for English as a Second Language (Hester, 1983; Garvie, 1990).

Egan (1988) sees stories as linguistic units which establish meaning, enabling children to feel with others or see through others' eyes. Since teaching is centrally concerned with organizing and communicating meaning, he advocates that teachers should develop story techniques for organizing events, facts or ideas into meaningful units. He outlines five steps for this. First, the teacher should identify important aspects of a curriculum topic and find something affectively engaging about it. Next, the teacher should find binary opposites that relate centrally to the topic (for example, change — stability, dependence — independence, survival — destruction), perhaps simplifying in the interests of making the topic accessible. Then the binary opposites are used to organize the curriculum content into a story form which embraces the opposites, using events, incidents or examples. After that, when the teacher teaches the topic, a resolution for the dramatic conflict inherent in the opposites is sought, to reach a satisfying conclusion. Finally, the teacher evaluates how it has been understood.

Gudmundsdottir (1990 and 1991) also sees teaching as creating meaning, usually out of texts. Teachers have to do this for themselves and they often make a story which organizes subject content for pedagogic purposes. She claims that the ability to do this is an important part of experienced teachers' pedagogical content knowledge — knowing how to restructure curriculum content for teaching purposes. Where Egan's (1988) proposals are aligned towards primary phases of schooling, Gudmundsdottir's research is concerned with teachers who are working in the secondary phase. She has worked with teachers of social sciences, history and literature. She observed them in the classroom and interviewed each five to seven times for up to two hours per interview. She found that experienced teachers often use a story as 'a solution to . . . the problem of how to translate knowing into telling' (White, 1981, p. 1). Large chunks of the curriculum are developed and dramatized, apparently according to a story schema, to make complex ideas more accessible and coherent. For example, a teacher of American history, teaching the subject matter chronologically, relates material to the recurring themes of the growth of opportunities, the age of discoveries, transformation or the clash of cultures (Gudmundsdottir, 1991, p. 213). Such themes, not unlike the images identified by Connelly and Clandinin

(1988), are elaborated and developed over many months. As with the images, teachers are probably not fully conscious of this use of narratives until they collaborate with a researcher.

Teachers' Anecdotes

One major limitation of the methods of narrative research in education which have been considered so far is that they usually deal with small samples of teachers. This is because autobiography, collaborative auto-biography, narrative inquiry and the curriculum stories approach involve protracted observation or extended interviewing with each teacher to explore the teacher's narrative to what is believed to be the necessary depth. The typical narrative research report centres around one or two cases, richly presented. As narratives, these mark out an area of the reader's consciousness and remain in memory. Thus Elbaz (1983) focusses on *Sarah*, Connelly and Clandinin (1986) present *Stephanie* and Gudmundsdottir (1990) introduces *Cathy* and *Chris*, while Pinar (1988) talks about himself. The research is peopled with individuals, each with his or her own voice, but do they speak for most teachers? These cases mediate our awareness of the method, but it can be questioned whether they mediate between the particular classroom and education in general, in one country, or in the West, or in the wider world.

A possible way to counter this difficulty is to notice that teachers spend a fair amount of their time talking to each other — 12 per cent of their working day, according to Hilsum (1972, p. 25), compared with 26 per cent of the day actually instructing pupils (Hilsum and Cane, 1971). A fair amount of this talk among colleagues consists of telling anecdotes about children and classroom events, or even about their own history as learners: 'Teachers often tell stories about their experiences as learners. They learn a great deal through reflecting, through their stories, on their experiences as children. They learn about teaching through reflecting on their experiences as learners' (Connelly and Clandinin, 1988b, p. 188).

The common occurrence of such naturally occurring narratives suggests that they might be readily gathered in substantially larger numbers than is normally possible using other narrative methods. Bennett (1983), for example, collected over 100 well-formed narratives told by college teachers in only six lunchtime gatherings in the staffroom. Cortazzi (1991, p. 9) recorded eighteen narratives in a fifty-minute discussion when nine primary headteachers considered the aims of education; four narratives when five primary headteachers spent two hours discussing mathematics curriculum guidelines; and four in each of two forty-minute discussions by teachers at a religious education conference. These are hardly contexts when one would expect extensive reminiscence. He also found that twenty-eight official staff meetings in one school, recorded over a year, contained sixty-four narratives, or slightly more than two per meeting on average. These were all anecdotes about classroom events.

The sheer frequency of these narratives, unprompted by researchers, suggests a method of gathering natural data among teachers' groups and staffrooms, or even in interviews, which has been developed by Cortazzi (1991). He has analyzed nearly 1000 such anecdotes, told by over 120 teachers, to give a broad cultural picture of teachers' perspectives. This research is reported in chapter 6. Here three further aspects of these anecdotes are worth comment.

First, such small stories of classroom incidents could easily be dismissed as 'anecdotal evidence'. They do not seem to carry the weight of the deeper, longer narratives collected in the biographic or curriculum-oriented methods. However, when 100 or so anecdotes told by as many teachers turn out to have a similar structure, telling of similar events, in the same order, using the same language, then it can be argued that such anecdotes, brief though some may be, do reflect important events, beliefs or attitudes of teachers. In short, they reveal key aspects of teachers' culture.

Second, it may be thought that such stories are decontextualized unless a researcher can observe the teller's classroom or ask him/her numerous background questions. However, further thought and investigation of narrative shows that naturally-occurring narratives necessarily contain sufficient context for listeners' correct interpretation. If not, the teller supplies it. At the least, they contain sufficient background — as perceived by the teller — for listeners to follow. If the researcher is interested in the teller's perceptions this is enough.

Third, many naturally occurring anecdotes are told among groups of teachers. If they clearly acknowledge or approve of a narrative then, in a sense, it belongs to all of them. Anecdotes told in staffrooms and elsewhere among groups may therefore have a strong social validity among teachers which other narrative data do not have. These themes are explored in chapter 2.

Further Factors in Narrative Research

There are a number of further factors to be considered. One is the critical relationship in collaborative biography or narrative inquiry between the researcher and the teacher. Ultimately, as Hastrup (1992) comments about fieldwork, 'It is not the unmediated world of the others but the world between ourselves and the others. Our results are deeply marked by this betweenness and there is no way, epistemologically, to overcome its implications (p. 117). Anthropologists working in the parallel relationship between anthropologist and informant have drawn attention to relevant factors. One of these is the role of the interviewer as a questioner and listener. As Okely (1992) remarks, 'The fashioning of oral autobiography, even before any written autobiography for specific readers, is affected by the listener's demands and shared readings' (p. 16). The teller is not the only person telling the tale. The listener also shapes the story. Questions, too, determine the direction and emphasis of the narrative. Even interviewer silence can have its meanings.

Another factor is the interviewer's notion of biography. A Western biographer or elicitor of autobiography may well be working within a cultural paradigm of a 'Great Man' tradition, where the story of a life is one of individual linear progress, a story of public achievement by a lone hero isolated from important social contexts, a story stressing the development of personality (Lejeune, 1974; Okely, 1992). After all, that is how the researcher has probably been socialized to think of biography, and the researcher's own biography also needs to be taken into account here. The history of Western autobiography is itself the history of the rise of the idea of individualism (Weintraub, 1978). Other peoples may not emphasize the individual at all; the social collective, the story of the group, may be what matters. Biography is a cultural construct that reflects fundamental assumptions about the nature of reality, attitudes and evaluations towards the self, time, nature and society.

Brumble's (1990) study of American Indian autobiography provides a salutory lesson. Early Indian autobiographies were as-told-to stories given in response to questioners, often through interpreters, written down by an amanuensis, then edited by a 'Western' editor. A common result was that two different assumptions about narrative were at work, two different senses of what it means to tell the story of one's life. The Western investigator sought turning points, key moments in the evolution of a unique self and how it came to be, asking about childhood events and arranging everything in a strict chronological order. The Indian narrators, in contrast, were conscious of their lives as the sum total of their adult deeds. They had a collective tribal sense of self. Childhood episodes were usually irrelevant. They were little concerned with chronology. They were what they had accomplished, the sum of their reputations. Consequently, their told narratives were likely to be discrete stories of episodes in a life, rather than the story of a life. The resulting written biography was often at best a distortion after editing, only corrected — if at all — after several generations of cultural misrepresentation.

Brumble (1990) quotes a revealing comment by a Western editor: 'Indian narrative style involves a repetition, and a dwelling on unimportant details which confuse the white reader and make it hard for him to follow the story. Motives are never explained ... Emotional states are summed up in such colourless phrases as "I liked it" ... For one not immersed in the culture, the real significance escapes' (p. 80).

But the Indian narrator's perspective is somewhat different: 'A lot of anthropologists, they come here and they say they want to be my friend, then they go away and put down what I say in books and make a lot of money' (*ibid*, p. 90).

Clearly the person of the researcher and his/her biography and presuppositions can make a difference. The race, age, gender, social and cultural background, and so on, of the teacher and the researcher, and the relationship between them must all be accounted for. Gender, for example, could make a difference, and this might pass unnoticed: 'There are differing narratives of the self; the "feminine" one being open to representing experience as interpersonal while the "masculine" one privileges individualism and distance' (Okely, 1992, p. 12).

If narrative, as a research or teacher training enterprise, is to be the critical emancipating exercise which some have advocated then it must include a reflexive element: not only about how the research was carried out, but also about what kind of people the researcher and teacher are, about *both* of their biographies, *both* of their sets of presuppositions, and about the nature of the relationship between them. This reflexive element should also include the research participants' ideas about the nature of the research — there is, after all, a culture of 'doing research' to be considered. Finally, as the example of early American Indian autobiography shows, the reflexive element must include participants' ideas about narrative itself, lest genre expectations are imposed without warrant. If we are to use narrative in a reflective approach to teacher development, we need to reflect on the nature of narrative.

The factor of narrative itself, that the nature of narrative can influence or determine the outcome of narrative-based research, seems obvious. Yet few researchers currently working with narrative in education and social sciences give explicit accounts of what narrative is and how narratives work, or what their presuppositions in this regard are.

As Atkinson (1990) comments, 'The ethnographic interview and the more casual fieldwork conversation are more or less deliberately contrived occasions when storytelling is facilitated . . . (yet) ethnographers have not paid a great deal of attention to the narrative qualities of the data they collect and report' (p. 104). One unexpected result is that ethnographic reports often contain autobiographical accounts of the researcher at work which are shaped by narrative structures into a pilgrim's progress type of account: 'The ethnographer presents him/herself as anti-hero, blundering and coping in strange and adverse circumstances . . . The story is often one of gaffes and near-misses . . . but these are written as things of the past, written in a period of naive misunderstanding before the enlightenment born of the fieldwork itself . . . they do not just have the wisdom of hindsight, but the hindsight born of hard-won wisdom' (*ibid*, pp. 106–8). Similar narrative conventions shape widely told types of teachers' stories, to the extent that the researcher may ask if the teacher is telling the story or whether the story is telling the teacher.

Gergen (1988) after a detailed study of life histories, concludes, 'People are only able to construe their lives within the confines of linguistic and social conventions' (p. 102). This means that narrative researchers need to know about and appreciate the limited vocabulary of forms of narrative; its literary conventions, even in oral stories; the social norms in which narratives are born and grow; the psychological context of narration; narrative as discourse and narrative as memory. We must know the limits and constraints — and the strong points — of the research methods in hand.

Some Conclusions

Recent research and thinking on reflection, teachers' knowledge and voice has led inexorably to the use of teachers' narrative. Narratives are increasingly being used as data and the narrative process is being used more and more as evidence for how teachers work. A wide range of basically narrative approaches are increasingly being used for teacher development, both in pre-service and in-service phases. Clearly they have much to offer for this purpose. In general, the research emphasizes how narratives play an important role in teachers' pedagogic development and career history and that narratives are key data for investigations of the teacher's world. However, the social, psychological and cultural roles of narrative in teachers' work, the structure and functions of narrative, have been underanalyzed.

As the concepts of 'narrative', 'story', 'biography', and so on, are being taken up by more and more researchers and practitioners in education and the social sciences there is a danger that their meaning will be overextended unwittingly to metaphoric uses far removed from the considered definitions of those who have developed narrative studies in other disciplines.

Narrative analysis is increasingly being used as research tool and yet the tool itself has been inadequately characterized in education. We must know what narratives are, how they work in the mind and how they function in the kind of social interactions involved in research interviews if we are to use them adequately for research purposes. An understanding of these aspects, derived from a range of disciplines which impinge on the field of narrative study, is vital if the current methodologies of narrative analysis are to be used on a wide scale in social and educational research. The next chapters address these questions in some detail.

Chapter 3

Sociological and Sociolinguistic Models of Narrative

Introduction

Sociological and sociolinguistic views of narrative have been developing since the 1960s but it is only recently that attention to these has been paid in education. There are four sections in this chapter. The first part looks at how conversation analysts find interactional patterns in the conversational context of narratives. In the second section, Goffman's comments on narratives are summarized, in the context of his dramaturgical model of face-to-face interaction. Labov's evaluation model of narrative is examined in the third section. This model focusses on the internal structure of narrative in a sociolinguistic context. The emphasis on the social context of narrative is taken further in the fourth section, in the work of Wolfson (1976) and Polanyi (1985), who link narrative with culture and performance respectively. This section specifically examines the interview context as a site for eliciting narratives.

Conversational Analysis and Narratives

Narratives which occur in natural oral settings have been examined from the perspective of Conversational Analysis. This perspective overlaps with that of ethnomethodologists who look at talk in order to try to understand how participants view their world. Researchers adopting these perspectives have shown that long stretches of apparently casual conversation are in fact highly structured and ask how this orderliness comes about. What social knowledge do people need to tell a narrative in conversation?

It is assumed that speakers are intuitively aware of certain rules of how to take part in conversation. They design their own contribution to fit the development of ongoing talk. They feel accountable for the interactional consequences of not following these rules. This is shown when speakers apologize for interrupting. Not to apologize would be to risk being thought of as inconsiderate or aggressive. Realizing in advance what constitutes an interruption, that they are interrupting and how others might interpret the interruption, speakers show their awareness of such social rules and expectations — and apologize first. Similarly, speakers adopt methodical solutions to the technical problem of how to introduce a narrative into turn-by-turn talk, making it a natural part of both prior and subsequent talk.

Thus Sacks (1972 and 1974), Jefferson (1978), Schegloff (1978), Ryave (1978) and Goodwin (1984) examine how narratives are constructed in the social organization of conversation. Compared with other models of narrative analysis, conversational analysis gives less attention to the internal structure of narrative. Rather, narrative is seen as an organized part of the ongoing sequence of talk, a dynamic production, jointly created by both teller and audience.

The Problem of Correct Interpretation

A fundamental methodological point made by conversational analysts is that the analyst can never have access to all the knowledge for interpretation which participants themselves have. However by examining the subsequent talk which follows a problematic utterance something of interactants' own interpretations can be seen from how they display their understanding of it through talk to each other. Often the immediate response shows the interpretation a second speaker makes of the preceding utterance. At other times the analyst may have to look over several exchanges in order to see what speakers have made of others' contributions (Labov and Fanshel, 1977, p. 352). Where recipients show a speaker that they have wrongly assessed the speaker's meaning, the speaker is likely to rephrase the original contribution or explicitly correct the recipient's reply. These subsequent comments by later speakers are not seen in a simple chaining relationship, but rather as an ongoing development of shared meaning which is revealed retrospectively by speakers in response to previous contributions. While the total interpretation remains elusive, the analyst has access to that part of interactants' understanding which they display to each other through talk.

The methodological strategy is therefore to track subsequent utterances, looking for internal evidence for the understanding displayed by conversational partners. Conversationalists are themselves analysts in this way, otherwise they would not be able to make sense out of talk (Levinson, 1983, p. 321). Analysts thus limit themselves to data to which interactants themselves have access (Schiffrin, 1988).

Turn-taking and Adjacency Pairs

Conversational analysts see narrative working within two linguistic systems. The first of these is *turn-taking*, how people take turns at talking. Sacks, Schegloff and Jefferson (1974) show how speakers' contributions are alternated and fitted into potential turn-taking positions in conversation, which they call 'transitional relevance points'. A transitional relevance point is not only the place in a conversation where there is a change of speaker but is also the point at which another participant has the right to speak, even if he/she chooses not to do so. This notion is used to explain how interruptions are recognized, where new speakers try to fit what they want to say into transitional relevance points but often time their contribution poorly and are heard as interrupting. The idea of a turn is also illustrated by the fact that there is a noticeable absence of a contribution when an expected turn is not taken up, as when someone fails to respond to a direct question. When taking a next turn a speaker shows how he/she understood the previous turn or turns. Turn-taking thus shows aspects of the structure of talk and of participants' understanding of rules for social interaction.

The second system is that of the *'adjacency pair'* (Sacks, 1973; Schegloff, 1972). This is a pair of utterances, produced successively by different speakers, which form an identifiable sequence. Thus an expression of *thanks* is commonly followed by an *acknowledgment*. A *complaint* may be followed by an *apology* or perhaps by a *justification* which seeks to show that there is no reason to complain. Such pairs are arranged back-to-back: given the first, the second is expected; when the second arises, it is interpreted as the completion of the first. For example, when an aggrieved person complains it is expected that the addressee will apologize. When an apology is given the person complaining knows that what was said has been understood as a complaint and that the complaint has been accepted. The first part (the complaint) has 'sequential implications' for the second part (the apology) by constraining a limited range of responses and if none of these appear this absence is noticeable and is interpreted accordingly. The second part is 'conditionally relevant' to the first, being interpreted as a type of utterance required by the first. Apologies only occur after certain types of utterances, such as complaints or insults. There will be a clear transitional relevance point between such adjacency pairs. Adjacency pairs can be seen as small linguistic systems. They can also be regarded as 'ritual interchanges' (Goffman, 1981, p. 17).

It is important to note that larger sequences can be built from adjacency pairs, that the second part shows a speaker's interpretation of the first part, and that not all adjacent turns are adjacency pairs (Schegloff, 1988, pp. 110–4). The use of adjacency pairs also varies cross-culturally. The above example illustrates a basic pattern. Conversation is often more complex than this. The apology in turn may be followed by an acceptance or mitigation ('That's all right'). The complaint itself may well be preceded by an apology ('I'm sorry to complain, but . . .'). Adjacency pairs thus often combine to form larger patterns.

Narratives as Turns

How are narratives organized within the structures of turn-taking and adjacency pairs? First, once a narrative is under way it effectively stakes out space to give the teller an abnormally long turn at talk. A narrative definitively wards off interruptions except to allow listeners to ask for something to be clarified or repeated. Such brief interruptions do not take the main turn away from the teller. They assist the teller to design the narrative to meet the knowledge and interest of listeners, and they elicit information which is required for the intended interpretation.

Since a narrative gives its teller a long turn, some speakers in discussions put their contributions in a narrative form in order to hold the floor for the maximum time, exercizing control or power and possibly introducing additional points which might otherwise be seen as irrelevant. Narratives give speakers strong rights to hold the floor.

Narratives in Conversational Sequences

Based on the work of Sacks (1972 and 1974) table 2 below can be constructed.

This model shows that narratives do not simply begin or end in conversation. They are methodically introduced into turn-by-turn talk. The audience is offered turns at structurally defined positions around a narrative and so narratives can be considered as joint speaker-audience productions. Narratives are part of a sequence of two adjacency pairs — the pre-sequence and sequence pair.

In table 2, 1 to 5 represent turns or, more exactly, a serially

Table 2: *The Conversational Sequencing of a Narrative*

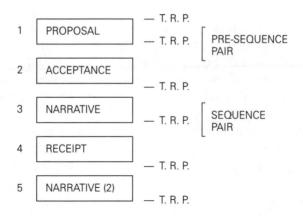

ordered set of structural positions in conversation. The conversational structures which give birth to narratives are precisely coordinated with mutual gaze, posture and other aspects of non-verbal communication (Goodwin, 1984, p. 236). Each structural position is separated by a transition relevance point (TRP) where normally any other speaker could take up a turn, following normal turn-taking rules (Sacks, Schegloff and Jefferson, 1974). However, it is in the nature of the Proposal at 1 that it suspends the usual turn-taking machinery and invokes a four-move conversation unit, 1–4, which cannot easily be interrupted legitimately.

Proposal

At 1, a speaker (A) takes up a turn and offers to tell a narrative, or requests a chance to tell one. ('I must tell you . . .' 'Have you heard about . . .?') This proposal is designed to achieve entry to a narrative and to get other participants to be an audience, or narrative recipients (Jefferson, 1978, p. 245). Narratives occupy unusually long turns and if they are simply begun without assent from the audience this could be seen as a sudden imposition or unwarranted control of talk. It is in the nature of narrative that the teller needs an audience, which implies participation. The Proposal is designed to elicit this participation in advance.

The Proposal establishes the newsworthiness or interest of the narrative, often by a preface (Sacks, 1974, p. 340) or abstract, which gives an idea of the narrative which will follow by summarizing its main point.

Acceptance

At 2, one or more speakers (B) accept the Proposal, signalling approval and acknowledging A's right to tell a Narrative ('No, I haven't heard.' 'Do tell me.' 'Oh yes, go on'). B will now take an audience role. Exceptionally, B may show mild disapproval ('Not another story.' 'Here he goes again.') or reject the Proposal ('I've heard that one before.' 'You've told me already.'), at the risk of offending A.

It can now be seen that A's Proposal is a neat move designed to get potential next speakers *not* to start talking (Schegloff, 1978, p. 94), but merely to give a minimal response to signal their Acceptance. This is not merely a 'one-step' setting-up (Goffman, 1975), where the first speaker selects the type of reply of the next speaker, but a two-step setting up. A's Proposal has selected not the next speaker, B, but rather the next but one, the proposer himself, A.

Turns 1 and 2 form a 'pre-pair' (Sacks, 1973) or 'pre-sequence' (Levinson, 1983, p. 349), i.e. an adjacency pair which is itself designed to be the gate to a second main pair, the Narrative and its Receipt.

Narrative

Speaker A now moves into the Narrative at turn 3, having negotiated the critical task of getting an extra long turn with the necessary co-operation of others. A has the floor for as long as the Narrative takes, since a narrative usually contains no transition relevance points. The Narrative itself pre-structures an extended turn, by virtue of the series of events to be recounted and because of its own internal structure. A still has the problem of telling an interesting story but is more or less assured of not being interrupted.

The audience, B, now have the interactional problem of listening, not only to the events, but for their significance (Ryave, 1978). They know that at the end of the Narrative there will be a transition relevance point, at 4, where they should show Receipt of the Narrative.

Receipt

At 4, B says something to acknowledge that the Narrative has been told, and may say something to show appreciation of the content or manner of the telling, or both (Goffman, 1981, p. 42, 148). Appreciation can also be an endorsement (Stubbs, 1983, p. 190) which will be significant for A ('Incredible!' 'Really?' 'Life's like that'). Realizing this fundamental need to show a Receipt, B will listen for when and how to react to the Narrative, while A will design the Narrative so that its point and its ending are clearly signalled. A will restrict the Narrative to facts and events which are relevant to the comments he intends to elicit, in order to aid B's Receipt.

It is in A's interest that there should be a Receipt (Moerman, 1973, p. 198). No teller is likely to offer a narrative unless he believes it will be accepted. The teller signals the end, but the Narrative is only complete when B accepts its completion (Schegloff, 1978, p. 94). B may demonstrate insufficient or variant understanding which A will feel obliged to remedy with clarification or correction. B can keep the Narrative going with questions, which A will have to deal with. All of this can take several additional turns, in the course of which A's telling will be perceived by B as being increasingly ineffective. Knowing this, A strives to achieve B's recognition of completion at the Receipt point by including all relevant information for a correct understanding. A helps B to react at the end, just as B helped A to begin.

In a sense, the narrative at 3 is 'ritually bracketted' (Goffman, 1981, p. 130) between A's Proposal and B's Acceptance — which are designed to achieve mutual recognition that the narrative may begin — and the Receipt — which shows that it is complete. The bracketting has the effect of transforming ordinary talk to a narrative context through 'keying' (*ibid*, p. 83), an effect which is mutually achieved and which will allow recognition of when and how the functions of narrative will operate.

Absence of Acceptance and Receipt

The Acceptance and Receipt both signal acceptance: that a Narrative will be told or that it has been told. However, there are differences which can be seen by considering the effect of their absence. The absence of the Acceptance at 2 commonly occurs. In such cases, sometimes the Proposal is repeated, and the delayed Acceptance may be accompanied by apologies or explanation for the delay (Schegloff, 1972). More usually A continues on with a Narrative, but only after a pause at the transition relevance point, giving B the right to a turn for a verbal Acceptance. This is expected, but need not be uttered. A rejection, as a marked form, would need to be uttered. B's silence thus signifies Acceptance by not taking the opportunity for a refusal.

The absence of a Receipt at 4, on the other hand, is dramatic. It is interpreted by A as showing either a lack of ackowledgment or a lack of understanding. In the first case A will probably repeat parts of the Narrative, for example, the ending, as a repeated exit device in a further attempt to elicit recognition of a completion from B (Jefferson, 1978, p. 245). In the second case A will probably repeat the point of the Narrative, or its evaluation, or add further detail to remedy what he now sees as B's lack of necessary information to understand. If in either case B's Receipt is still not forthcoming A's talking will probably tail off into a silence, in which he understands, as B does, that the Narrative has failed. This silence is embarrassing for both A and B since it can be interpreted as both a teller's deficiency in telling and as a recipient's lack of understanding (Sacks, 1974, p. 346).

Once a narrative has begun it is in everybody's interests that it should be seen to a successful completion. Both A and B will feel accountable for failure. Participants expect comments at 4, notice their absence, interpret that absence and do something about it (Moerman, 1973, p. 201).

Clearly, narratives in conversations are cooperative efforts. The weft of the narrator's contribution cannot easily be woven into turn-by-turn talk without the woof of the audience's participation.

A Series of Narratives

Position 5 in table 2 can now be considered. This could be a continuation of B's talk, following the Receipt and bridging the possible turn, or the turn could revert back to A. Either speaker can use the transition relevance point to take up another topic, since they are now free of the structural constraints which applied to positions 1–4.

More interestingly, second, or further Narratives, often appear at 5. Once one Narrative has been told, others may be anticipated, triggered off by the first. These can arise without the pre-sequence pair, speakers having now entered a narrative cycle of extended turns whose product may be a series of narratives by different speakers or by the same person.

Audience Receipts commonly intersperse a series of Narratives, but often these are not evident as such. The reason for the apparent absence of a Receipt under these circumstances is that a second Narrative itself functions as a Receipt, both acknowledging the first and showing appreciation of it, giving the strongest possible endorsement by telling the same kind of thing (Moerman, 1973, p. 206; Goffman, 1981, p. 206).

Later Narratives are highly pre-specified, showing marked parallels of topic, theme, character of events with preceding Narratives. Subsequent Narratives stand in an adjacency relationship with previous Narratives: they display their teller's understanding of these previous Narratives. There is the further possibility that first tellers can respond in a Receipt slot to second Narratives, either commenting on the second as such or commenting on the second as a response to the first. We can conclude that a series of Narratives is not simply a chain but is rather a sequenced ongoing mutual creation between participants with alternating speaker–audience roles.

Interpretations in a Series of Narratives

The interpretation of Receipts and of second and later Narratives gives analysts using a transcript interactants' interpretations of what the point of the first Narrative was, since what the teller of the second Narrative took the first to be about is on record (Moerman, 1973, p. 206). Also on record is how the first teller, through a Receipt, took both the second Narrative and the second teller's interpretation of the first.

When participants make their understanding explicit in this way it is often focussed even more by a further factor, that second tellers frequently feel the need to cap the efforts of first tellers. Subsequent Narratives often exaggerate the point of prior Narratives.

From this, table 3 can be constructed showing a hall-of-mirrors reflection of interpretations of a Narrative, N1, assuming that subsequent speakers and tellers agree about the point and show their agreement via Receipts and subsequent Narratives, N2, N3.

Of course, there may be disagreement on the interpretation of the first narrative by other speakers, giving the modified model shown in table 4.

In either of the two cases, of subsequent agreement or disagreement, the narratives in such a series share a relationship beyond mere sequential adjacency (Ryave, 1978). Subsequent narratives are related by topic and/or setting. Each teller may figure as the principle character in his/her narrative and steers that narrative to, or from, the significance (evaluative point) of the preceeding narrative. Narratives become interactional resource material for subsequent narrators.

In cases of agreement, participants telling second or later narratives show **in** and **through** their narrative **that** and **how** they understand the preceeding narrative (*ibid*). In cases of disagreement, recipients show their disagreement with the immediately preceeding narrative, while implicitly or explicitly reinforcing the significance of the last-but-one narrative.

Table 3: A Series of Narratives with Agreed Interpretation

SPEAKER	NARRATIVE/ RESPONSE	STATE OF INTERPRETATION
A	N1	— tells narrative
B	Receipt	— shows acceptance/understanding of N1
B/other	N2	— shows endorsement of N1. If teller = A, shows endorsement of B's Receipt
A/other	Receipt	— by A, teller of N1, shows acceptance of N2 and of N2 teller's interpretation of N1. By another, shows appreciation of N2 reflecting N1
C/other	N3	— shows endorsement of N2, and of N2's interpretation of N1
A/other	Receipt	— shows acceptance of N3, and of N3's interpretation of N2's interpretation of N1.

Table 4: A Series of Narratives without Agreed Interpretation

SPEAKER	NARRATIVE/ RESPONSE	STATE OF INTERPRETATION
A	N1	— tells narrative
B	Receipt	— accepts telling, but with misunderstanding or disagreement
B	N2	— illustrates disagreement with a counter-narrative
A	Receipt	— accepts telling, but with misunderstanding or disagrees with the point of N2
A	N3	— reemphasizes N1, a counter-counter-narrative to N2
B	Receipt	— accepts telling, but probably reverts to interpretation of N2. May follow with yet another narrative.

Criticisms of Conversational Analysis

Conversational analysis has been the subject of a number of criticisms. Descriptive categories are not defined, form is insufficiently related to function, neither data nor categories are exhaustively analyzed, intonation and paralanguage are insufficiently taken into account (Coulthard, 1977, p. 91; Taylor and Cameron, 1987). Moreover, turns and adjacency pairs are not the most relevant basic units (Goffman, 1981, but see Schegloff, 1988, for a reply); there is no explicit method of moving from the narrative text to an understanding of its significance in conversation (Polanyi, 1981b); there may be cross-cultural variation in valuing and using turns; and that informal conversation may not be the basic form of speech exchange systems (Corsaro, 1985).

Some of these criticisms can be acknowledged but they may not be relevant to analyzing teachers' narratives. Others, such as cultural variation, will be discussed in chapter 5.

Implications of Conversational Analysis for Teachers' Narratives

For an analysis of teachers' narratives it is useful to track subsequent talk and to look for the Receipt. This will show participants' own interpretations of narratives. This is also useful to remember in an interview situation where the interviewer is a participant, as long as he/she reacts as a recipient to teacher talk and not merely as a questioner. The interview transcript may show the interviewer's reaction to a teacher's narrative and the teacher's response to that reaction. Examining the Receipt in this way becomes a validation procedure.

It is useful to recognize that teachers' narratives are often located in pairs of adjacency pairs. Looking at an interview transcript one can often see how narratives are cooperatively produced in the sequential organization of conversation. The organization of a teacher's narrative (not its content) is not a solo effort. When positively received in a group of teachers, a narrative belongs to the group, as a common sociocultural product.

Second and later narratives are interesting in their own right and as interpretations of first narratives. The cumulative agreement about the meaning of a series of narratives is likely to be powerful evidence of a group of teachers' perceptions, ideas and cultural values.

It can be seen that a narrative, once begun, guarantees the teller an extended turn at talk. This may be used by some teachers to control turns in informal talk or in formal discussions and meetings. Some teachers intuitively know this; a chairperson, headteacher or discussion leader may preempt, shorten or build on narratives in academic settings, conferences, or teachers' meetings to control talk. Knowledge of how narratives are born in interaction may also help research interviewers who wish to elicit stories from teachers.

An Example

An example of such a series of teachers' narratives follows. The narrators are headteachers at a conference discussing religious education (RE), which is a part of the British National Curriculum. There were twenty-three headteachers in the group.

N1

A   I'm surprised to hear you say that most teachers use a traditional Bible approach rather than a thematic approach. Many teachers are reacting against using Bible stories. When I was in the primary school, I remember the head, a very stern man, he stood out at the front and said Psalms. 'I life mine eyes up to heaven . . .' It was an authoritarian society. I think we probably accepted it at the time, but we reacted against it at the age of 19. Now as teachers we are still reacting against it and not using Bible stories.

N2

B   Well, I was reminded about a lesson at primary school when I was there. We had this lesson about sharing. It was a story about a couple of boys. These boys shared something and then the teacher brought it home with a Bible story. I still remember it now, so some traditional RE teaching must be effective.

N3

And another thing, I always remember from when I was a class teacher we were talking about God and this boy said, 'I don't know much about God, but He's very beautiful.' I quote that one a lot in service — I'm a lay preacher.

Speaker A presents his narrative (N1) about the Psalm-saying headteacher as a personal experience of reacting against traditional Bible approaches. N1 is sandwiched between generalizations, when the speaker already has the floor. It is used to support an argument about social change.

N2 is triggered off by N1, 'I was reminded about a lesson ...' It acts as a Receipt to N1, endorsing the telling, showing understanding, but not endorsing the point of N1. N2 sustains the theme of childhood experience, but shows the opposite effect of N1. This counter-narrative contains two implied narratives, 'a story about a couple of boys' and 'a Bible story' which are unelaborated. N2 leads to N3 with 'and another thing'. The relevance of the point of N3, the boy's comment about the nature of God, to the previous discussion seems unclear. Perhaps B, having got the floor, wishes to keep his turn and ward off potential speakers with a further narrative. Both speakers refer to personal childhood experience rather than to theory, analysis or logical argumentation. This might be interpreted as showing the influence of teachers' own experience as pupils on their thinking now as teachers. By affirming the validity of their experiences as pupils, even to illustrate opposite viewpoints, A and B may be implying that they and their listeners, as teachers, potentially influence children they teach in similar ways. B's second narrative also shows how teachers may learn from children.

Narratives as Replayings of Personal Experience

This next section considers Goffman's model of Frame Analysis (1975), which like conversational analysis has its sociological origins in ethnomethodology. Goffman's sociology is broadly concerned with how people organize face-to-face interaction. He uses an elaborate dramaturgical metaphor to draw parallels between the stage and conversation. His work includes scattered insightful comments on conversational narratives, mostly to be found in 'Frame Analysis'.

Goffman uses five concepts — of 'self', 'ritual', 'face', 'performance' and 'frame' — to see narratives as 'replayings' of 'strips of activity'. Each of these will be considered briefly and related to Goffman's view of narratives.

Self

Following Mead (1934), Goffman sees a person's *self*, not as a private, individual attribute, but as a socialized entity, created in and through social interaction. In this view, narrative is self-expression, but it involves the management of information about the self: impression-management through conversational rituals. Interaction is a process of exchange of impressions or self-presentations between ritually enacted selves, where each participant relies on others to complete his picture of his own self (Collins, 1988, p. 49).

Ritual and Face

Conversation further involves two sets of requirements: those of *system* and *ritual* (Goffman, 1981, p. 14). The system requirements consist of constraints on basic organization, of the kind described by conversational analysts. The ritual requirements, underestimated by conversational analysts, describe the moral character, the reciprocally-held norms of good and proper conduct which govern ways of negotiating narrative in talk through ritualization (Kendon, 1988, p. 31 and 37). Narrative will thus be organized around the presentation of the teller's proper or desirable self (Goffman, 1969; Polanyi, 1982a, p. 519) and around the preservation of his *'face'* in situations of difficulty or embarrassment. Audiences will also show a similar concern to maintain both the teller's and their own face throughout a narrative. Face is the motivational basis for the ritual organization of interaction.

Multiple-selves

However, the social self, displayed to best advantage, is not viewed as a single entity. Goffman presents the notion of multiple-selfing in narrative (Goffman, 1975, p. 517 and 1981, p. 144). He distinguishes the teller as the *author*, the self who composes the lines; as the *principal*, the self as protagonist, 'the party to whose position the words attest'; and as the *animator*, the self as emitter, 'the sounding box' producing utterances, facial expressions and gestures. Levinson (1983, p. 170) adds further distinctions between *source*, the origin of the words, and speaker, so that the author is both source and speaker, but a *relayer* is a speaker who is not the source. This is a useful distinction with which to discuss quoted dialogue in narrative (see chapter 4).

Performance

The animator of a narrative effectively gives a *'performance'*, a notion emphasizing the on-the-spot attempt to influence the audience through impression management (Goffman, 1969, p. 26). The performer is 'a harried fabricator of impressions' (*ibid*, p. 244) narrating about characters, including the teller as principal, whose sterling qualities the performance is designed to emphasize. Where the performance of a narrative highlights common official values of the social group of teller and audience it can be viewed as a ceremony, an 'expressive rejuvenation', or a 'reaffirmation of the moral values of the community' (*ibid*, p. 45). When the expressive nature of performance is accepted, it has characteristics of celebration. These notions add richness to our perception of the sociocultural value of narrative performance (see chapter 5).

Talk, especially through performance, defines situations, marking off activities from the flow of surrounding events (Goffman, 1975, p. 25). However, Goffman emphasizes that each participant can be in complex layers of definitions of the situation at the same time. The social world can be transformed through a shifting of frames in talk.

Frames

'*Frames*' are socially-defined realities, 'principles of organization' which govern social events and our subjective involvement in them (*ibid*, p. 10). They are both of the social world and participants' response to it, sustained in activity and in the mind. Frames are therefore operating during narration both by framing the social events narrated in schemata of interpretation and by evaluating those events subjectively in the viewing of them during the process of narrative performance. The audience's viewing as participants in performance means that they too are also part of an external performance frame. Adjacency pairs can then be seen as a mutually organized framing into and out of narrative.

Narratives as Replaying of Experience

Narratives are defined by Goffman (1981) as being tapes or 'strips of personal experience' from the teller's past which are 'replayed' (p. 174). These strips are presented not as mere reporting, but as something to reexperience (Goffman, 1975, p. 506) and the reexperiencing is not only for the teller but also for the audience so that they can empathetically insert themselves into the replaying, vicariously experiencing what took place.

The performance of such a replayed strip of personal experience necessarily means maintaining suspense for the audience, keeping them ignorant of the outcome of the narrative, but wanting to know it. Even if the audience has been told the outcome in the Preface to the narrative, they must suspend this knowledge and be led through the path of discovery by a teller who must himself know the outcome, but will tell the narrative as if he too does not know it.

As principal protagonist, the teller takes listeners back to the state of knowledge he had at the time of the episode, but no longer has. Narration thus involves a framing away from present reality and present knowledge, running through a strip of already determined events as if the outcome were unknown. The outcome is unknown not only to those persons hearing, but also to those narrating and those narrated about (see chapter 4).

The Role of the Audience

Since narration is all about performance — the staging of a presentation of self — what matters is not whether it has been told before but whether it has been heard before. 'Effective performance requires first hearings, not first tellings' (*ibid*, p. 508), so the teller borrows spontaneity from the audience, for whom this is a first hearing.

The role of the audience is to show appreciation (Receipt). What is narrated in performance is not said *to* the audience, but *for* it. 'They are to be stirred not to take action, but to exhibit signs that they have been stirred' (*ibid*, p. 503). The narrator does not seek shouts of responsive action, but 'seeks to get murmurings — the clucks and tusks and aspirated breaths, the goshes and gollies and wows — which testify that the listener has been stirred, stirred by what is being replayed for him' (*ibid*, p. 541). This feedback is vital to tellers, otherwise listeners are seen as mere hearers. 'No audience, no performance' (*ibid*, p. 125). Tellers know they must perform and they know audiences know this. Narratives are designed to get to an 'appreciation of a show put on' (*ibid*, p. 547).

Quoting in Narrative

Much of the vivid performance of replaying comes from quoting others' words. Here the teller acts out another, typically in a mannered voice so that the quoted strip uses not only the other's words but carries tone, gestures and facial expressions to categorize, but not to impersonate, the quoted figure. This is the animator at work and it requires further framing. The performance may be so convincing that narrators do not even need verbs of reporting as frames within the narrative (She said, replied, remarked, etc.). An example of this occurred when a teacher dramatically quoted herself thinking in the middle of a narrative about a child learning to read. The teacher said in her narrative, 'Recently I've seen, "Yes, it's there. At last you can do it." '

The teller speaks *for* others, apparently *in* their words (Goffman, 1981, p. 145). Yet tellers often shift their focus from *what* people in the narrative actually said (as sources) to the sort of thing they *would* say, in such circumstances (*ibid*, p. 43). Here the narrator is effectively a hypothetical relayer of the typical rather than of the actual.

There seems to be a balance in many narratives between typicality and uniqueness, or between the normal and the dramatic. Sacks (1984, p. 419) notes that dramatic narratives are sometimes played down to give a 'nothing much happened' sense, either to prevent a narrative being dismissed as outrageous fabrication, or in Goffman's terms to protect loss of face by presenting the narrator as one so competent that the dramatic can be treated as ordinary.

The apparent vivid spontaneity of performance should not cause an analyst to lose sight of the prefabricated (Goffman, 1981, p. 504), pre-formulated nature of narrative. Narratives are always organized from the beginning in terms of what will prove to be the outcome (*ibid*, p. 559) (see chapter 4).

This pre-formulation is, of course, also constrained, first by the linearity of speech and second by the temporal sequencing of narrative events, where real-world simultaneity cannot be replayed in a narrative. Narrators must inevitably transform (Labov, 1972 and 1981), and plan to transform, the complexity of the reality of what happened into a single strip for replaying ('this is what I am able to tell you about the sequence of what happened').

It is a considerable accomplishment to bring all this to bear in telling a narrative in conversation.

Criticisms of Goffman's Approach

There are criticisms of Goffman's approach, which can be summarized as an equivocal attitude to data, imprecision in the use of concepts, and unacknowledged cultural limitations (Drew and Wootton, 1988).

However, none of these criticisms seem to detract from the relevance of Goffman's insights for a study of teachers' narratives.

Implications of Goffman's Frame Analysis for the Analysis of Teachers' Narratives

There are a number of insights from Frame Analysis which are applicable to teachers' narratives. The emphasis on the interdependence of participants in face-to-face interaction, their mutual monitoring and the joint production of teachers' narratives by both teller and audience, which reinforce the notion of cultural perspectives between researcher and teacher. Yet there are many 'as ifs' in teacher narration: events are framed in a linear fashion as if representing real events; within a narrative protagonists' perspectives and words are presented as if they see and say things that way; the event sequence is recounted as if the outcome were not known; teachers' narratives are told as if they are spontaneous instead of being preformulated. These 'as ifs' reinforce the idea that teachers' narratives do not necessarily reflect classroom reality, though they may refract teachers' perspectives. This is an advantage for the researcher wishing to investigate such perspectives.

Teachers' narratives of personal experience can be thought of as impression-management, as the presentation of their professional selves. Narratives of disasters may be presented in such a way as to preserve face. Narratives of successful children's learning may reveal a complex interweaving of the professional face of the expert versus the personal face of humility. These self-presentations might be considered part of the management of professionals. In narrative performance teachers are enacting their professional selves and in doing so are coming to know their own and others' selves, framed in the sociocultural contexts of classroom events.

Goffman's consistent dramaturgical metaphor emphasizes roles, staging, the presentation of self and performance. In the ritualized theatricality of performing a strip of past experience, primary teachers as narrators are both actors and storytellers: this is manifestly true in the classroom — in narrative it is also true in the staffroom. This theatricality is further shown in narrative performance when teachers act out children's roles in dialogue, often alternating between teacher and pupil and presenting a child-self as well as a teacher-self in multiple frames. This seems to be a way for experienced teachers to demonstrate how well they know children.

The dramaturgical metaphor is also bound up with ritual and ceremony. Staffroom story sessions may have ritualized, ceremonial, celebratory aspects which by confirming cultural and social belonging combats the isolation of much primary teaching.

Labov's Evaluation Model of Narrative

This model will be the basis for the analysis of narratives in chapter 6, enriched by the concepts presented in this chapter and supplemented by insights from chapters 3, 4 and 5.

Background

Labov's model of narrative analysis is a sociolinguistic approach which examines formal structural properties of narratives in relation to their social functions. Labov and his co-workers (Labov and Waletsky, 1967) originally developed particular interview questions in sociolinguistic research in order to overcome the formal constraints of face-to-face interviews. Some questions seemed to obtain more casual, natural speech because speakers became more personally involved with what they were saying. For example, the Danger of Death question: 'Were you ever in a situation where you were in serious danger of being killed, where you said to yourself, "This is it"?'; or the Fight question: 'Were you ever in a fight with someone bigger than you?' Such questions elicited oral narratives of personal experience and deeply involved speakers in rehearsing or reliving events in their past (Labov, 1972, p. 354).

Labov's initial purpose was to correlate the informal speech styles of narrative with social variables. Later, narratives were analyzed in their own right in terms of their structure and social function, which were correlated with the age, social class and ethnicity of narrators.

Narrative Clauses and Free Clauses

Labov defines a narrative as a means of representing or recapitulating past experience by a sequence of ordered sentences that match the temporal sequence of the events which, it is inferred, actually occurred (*ibid*, p. 359). A minimal narrative is a sequence of two clauses which are temporally ordered so that reversing their order reverses the temporal sequence of the original semantic interpretation (*ibid*, p. 360).

This definition presents narrow criteria for a narrative, but it enables the analyst to distinguish between narrative clauses and free clauses. *Narrative clauses* are in the past tense (occasionally in present tenses), temporally ordered with respect to each other, separated by 'temporal juncture'. The order of the clauses cannot be altered without changing the inferred sequence of events in the original semantic interpretation.

Free clauses, in contrast, can be rearranged or redistributed in a narrative sequence without unduly altering the semantic interpretation (Labov and Waletsky, 1967, p. 21).

Functions of Narrative

Labov develops a *formal* analysis based on recurrent patterns, which examines invariant structural units, and a *functional* analysis which puts forward two social functions of narrative, 'referential' and 'evaluative' (*ibid*, p. 33). The *referential* function of a narrative is to give the audience information through the narrator's recapitulation of experience, in the same order as the occurrence of the original events. This would be a straightforward report of what occurred. Labov maintains that speakers rarely give such a report. They evaluate the events. The *evaluative* function is to communicate to the audience the meaning of the narrative by establishing some point of personal involvement. This is what makes the narrated events reportable and 'without the concept of reportability we cannot begin to understand the things that people do in telling narratives' (Labov *et al*, 1968, p. 30). This function is a crucial element of narrative, so much so that the model will be termed hereafter the *'Evaluation model'* to draw attention to the way tellers give their perspective on the narrative content by evaluating the meaning it has for them. Evaluation is a natural, even unconscious, part of narration.

Narrative Structure

Labov suggests that a fully formed oral narrative of personal experience has a six part structure (Labov and Waletsky, 1967, p. 32; Labov, 1972, p. 363). These parts can be viewed as answers to audience questions, as shown in table 5. Each element in the structure is examined below.

Abstract

The Abstract is optional. When it occurs, it initiates the narrative by summarizing the point or by giving a statement of a general proposition which the narrative will exemplify. It signals the start of the narrative by past tense reference (like the Proposal in conversation analysis). Abstracts do not replace narratives, since the teller has no intention of stopping at this point. The Abstract is important because it conveys

Table 5:   The Structure of Narrative in the Evaluation Model

STRUCTURE	QUESTION
ABSTRACT	— What was this about?
ORIENTATION	— Who? When? What? Where?
COMPLICATION	— Then what happened?
EVALUATION	— So what?
RESULT	— What finally happened?
CODA	

general propositions which often go beyond the immediate events in the narrative.

Orientation

The Orientation or Setting typically gives details of time, persons, place and situation. This is the background which the teller believes the audience requires to understand the narrated events. Narratives contain their own context, provided in sufficient detail by tellers for the narrative to be understood without further knowledge of the characters and their situation. If a narrative is isolated from a conversation it will generally be self-contained as far as this context is concerned, unless the teller knows the audience is already familiar with the background. Certainly in interviews the Orientation gives the necessary and sufficient context. Orientation information is encoded in free clauses, usually placed at the beginning, sometimes coupled with the first event of the Complication. The Orientation does not contain information which is in itself reportable. Past progressive tenses are often used to sketch the activity that was in progress before the first event. The Orientation can, however, refer to a past event with an adverb of time which will mark off the narrative from previous talk, as an initiating mechanism. This leads to Labov and Fanshel's (1977, p. 106) formulation of a rule of Narrative Orientation which confirms the interactive nature of narrative beginnings. For a speaker A addressing a hearer B:

If A makes reference to an event that occurred prior to the time of speaking, which cannot be interpreted by any rule of discourse as a complete speech action in itself then B will hear this reference as the Orientation to a narrative to follow.

On hearing the Orientation B will cede the floor to A for an extended narrative turn.

Complication

The Complication follows the Orientation and consists of a series of narrative clauses in the past simple tense, or sometimes in present tenses, using the so-called historical present. This part of the narrative, the bones of it, gives the event sequence which is often terminated by the Result. Usually the Complication shows a turning-point, a crisis or problem, or a series of these. At the very least, it must present an event of interest. Sometimes the Complication is an extended section. It is basically the content of the narrative.

Evaluation

The Evaluation commonly precedes the Result. It 'delays the forward movement of the narrative at a certain point by the use of many non-narrative clauses, which hold the listener suspended at that point in time' (*ibid*, p. 108). The Evaluation is 'the means used by the narrator to indicate the point of the narrative, its *raison d'être*, why it was told' (Labov, 1972, p. 366). It avoids the withering rejoinder from listeners of 'So what?' since 'every good narrator is continually warding off this question' (*ibid*). The Evaluation highlights the point of the narrative, tells recipients why it was told and 'reveals the attitude of the narrator towards the narrative by emphasizing the relative importance of some narrative units as opposed to others' (Labov and Waletsky, 1967, p. 37). 'Narratives do not merely inform: they convey the importance of the narrated events and tell how those events should be interpreted and weighed by the listener' (Peterson and McCabe, 1983, p. 60). The absence of an Evaluation is exceptional in oral narratives of personal experience, though not in narratives of vicarious experience. 'Unevaluated narratives lack structural definition' (Labov and Waletsky, 1967, p. 39). The Evaluation is realized by a number of evaluative devices listed below which can be distributed at various points throughout a narrative, although they are commonly positioned before the Result. The Evaluation is a kind of self-Receipt through which the speaker gives the meaning of the narrative. It is a signal as to how the teller intends that others should receive the telling.

Result

The Result or resolution, as the term implies, describes the result or resolution to a conflict in the narrative. It follows the Complicating Action or Evaluation.

Coda

An optional Coda finishes the narrative by returning listeners to the present moment. It marks the close, often by using a formula such as 'That was it' which brackets the narrative as a point in the past the telling of which is now over. In the previous diagram the Coda had no corresponding question since it finishes the narrative, putting off such questions by announcing 'I've finished'. The Coda reinstates normal turn-taking mechanisms.

It is vital for listeners to recognize the Evaluation since they are expected to respond to it by a Receipt. The 'most general characterization' of the place of narrative in conversation is that 'it is given as an instance of a general proposition' (Labov and Fanshel, 1977, p. 109) with which listeners must agree or disagree.

Evaluation Devices

The Evaluation model is central to the investigation presented in chapter 6, so more details of the Evaluation are now given. Labov and others (Labov, 1972, pp. 370–5; Peterson and McCabe, 1983, p. 222) give a comprehensive list of the Evaluation devices. These often show syntactic complexity where the narrative clauses show syntactic simplicity. It is important to note that in principle the Evaluation must stand out from the norm of the narrative text and that almost *any* element *can* act evaluatively, by drawing attention to itself, by being linguistically marked. This principle explains the enormous variety of the devices listed below.

External Evaluation: this is where the narrator interrupts the narrative to step outside the recounting to tell listeners what the point is. There are five degrees of embedding in external evaluation. In increasing order of embeddedness these are: the narrative is interrupted while the teller says *explicitly* what the point is; in the narrative an interpretive remark is attributed to *narrator* as a principal, addressing himself at the time; the narrator as principal quotes himself as *addressing other characters*; an interpretive remark is *attributed to any other character* in the narrative; narrating an *evaluative action*: what characters did rather than what they said ('he turned white', 'she was shaking like a leaf'). Labov claims that the first three are common in the narratives told by middle class narrators while the last two are used by lower classes (Labov, 1972, p. 371).

Internal Evaluation: here the evaluation is internal to sentences and thus more embedded in the narrative texture. A wide variety of lexical, syntactic, phonological, and paralinguistic devices are used (Labov, 1972, p. 378; Polanyi, 1982b, p. 516). Labov puts these into the four groups. First there are *intensifiers*, which emphasize a specific event among a chain of narrative events: modifiers (adjectives, adverbs); quantifiers (adverbs); wh-exclamations (why! where!); repeated lexical items; gestures; heightened stress; vowel lengthening; and wide variation in intonation and pitch range. Second are *comparators*: use of negatives and modal verbs to refer to events which did not occur, but which might have occurred; questions embedded in the action; use of or-clauses; imperatives; future tenses; and comparatives and superlatives (adjectives, adverbs). Thirdly there is *extension*, which brings together two events conjoining them in a single independent clause: progressives; appended participles; double appositives; and doubling in attributes (adjectives). Finally there are *explications* or explanations: causal or qualifying subordinate clauses embedded within an independent clause.

The Evaluation Model is widely referred to and has been applied in literary analysis (Platt, 1977; Carter and Simpson, 1982; Maclean, 1988); in education, for analyzing children's writing (Taylor, 1986; Wilkinson, 1986); in developmental psycholinguistics (Kernan, 1977; Peterson and McCabe 1983); in mass communications (van Dijk, 1984, 1988a and 1988b); and in anthropology (Watson, 1972). However there are two levels of criticism which can be made.

Criticisms of the Evaluation Model

First, the isolation of the Evaluation devices is difficult because of the the lack of a one-to-one relationship of any particular structure with the evaluation function (Kernan, 1977, p. 100). The Evaluation section as a structural slot often appears between the Complicating Action and Result, but Labov draws a wave diagram (1972, p. 369) to show that Evaluative devices are distributed throughout the narrative. With so many devices and so few constraints on distribution, the analyst is seeking both a structure in, and a function of, the narrative, with little in the way of a discovery procedure. This criticism can be offset by reference to the linguistic principle of marking — the Evaluation devices stand out in contrast to the surrounding narrative text. Since most anecdotes come across to audiences successfully it is clear that if listeners can get the point the analyst can do so. In addition, an investigator could support an Evaluation analysis by looking for '*lexical signalling*' as explained below.

The second level of criticisms stems from other disciplines or fields outside sociolinguistics: conversational analysis, literary criticism, psychology and anthropology. Conversation analysts look for the place of narrative in the social organization of conversation. Labov does not consider this. Literary critics find Labov's definition of a narrative too strict, because his criterion of the temporal ordering of clauses rules out flashbacks, flashforwards, embedding and subordination, which are common in literary narrative (Toolan, 1988, p. 181). The obvious counterargument, that this is a sociolinguistic model not a literary one, is weakened when the Evaluation model is directly applied to achronic narrative. Cognitive psychologists see the Evaluation model as surface oriented. It makes no reference to cognitive structures or processes, although it has been used in developmental psycholinguistics (Petersen and McCabe, 1983). Anthropologists may see the Evaluation model as being culturally specific, since Labov has only correlated narrative functions and structures with age, social class and ethnicity in the United States. These criticisms can be met by taking literary, psychological and anthropological approaches to narrative into account, which substantially strengthens the model.

Some Examples

N4

A   They are so funny some of the things the children say.

O   I remember in my very first year of teaching — those were the days when they wrote a story on a piece of paper and if it was nicely done they would sit and very carefully write it down in their best book— and I remember having forty-four children in my class and trying to hear reading and give words to somebody else and children coming up to me to say, 'Where do I do this?' and I was saying, 'Do it on paper. Do it on paper.'

C   and up comes a child and I say, 'Do it on paper.'

R   and he looks at me very surprised and says, 'But I want to go to the toilet, Miss.'

Coda   That remains in my mind.

E   We get frustrated at times but we've had all sorts of funny things here. I thoroughly enjoy my job and find lots of things I can laugh at.

The structure of the narrative can be analyzed, using the abbreviations A, O, C, R, Coda and E for the categories of the Evaluation model. Each narrative can be analyzed as a whole for its content and cultural perspectives. Alternatively, parts of it, such as the Evaluation, could be compared with similar structures of other narratives on the same topic.

In this example the Abstract gives a general statement about classroom humour from the teacher's point of view. The Orientation specifies a distant time reference and outlines the procedure for copying out good work, no longer this teacher's current practice. This is necessary background to appreciate the 'Do it on paper' remark. The mention of the large class size is crucial, since together with the listed range of activities in progress, it gives a clear picture of rapid and constant teacher-pupil interactions. The teacher's formula for coping with the queue of children, 'Do it on paper', and the constant interruptions of the reading add to the picture of business, later interpreted as frustration. The switch to the narrative present, 'up comes a child', which is maintained for the subsequent chain of main verbs dramatizes the Complication. The Evaluation emphasizes the humour and enjoyment of teaching. Clearly the teacher was able to laugh at the incident. The overall perspective can be summarized: Teaching can be frustrating because with large classes it is difficult to organize many activities simultaneously whilst giving individual attention. (The teller shows that she presumes that this is the accepted manner of organizing classroom work.) However, children say funny things and the teacher enjoys her job partly because of the ability to find things to laugh at. Humour and enjoyment predominate over frustration.

In the next example the teacher has just been asked if he has had trouble with parents.

N5

O   One occasion ... the one occasion that does stick in my mind was last year. We had a fair bit of snow at one time and I decided to do a bit of creative writing from it and I thought I'd take the kids out into it, just to walk around and listen to the snow crunching under their feet and so on, and take it from there

C   and I sort of said to them, I sort of thought, 'It's asking for trouble, someone's going to start throwing snow around', so I said, 'If anybody starts playing about with the snow I shall bury them in it', you know, and of course one of them inevitably did throw a snowball at somebody else, so I thought, 'Well, I've got to do something, having said I'll do something', so I just picked up a ball of snow and I just went CLASH! on his head, you see, and some of it inevitably dripped down his neck and apparently at break time, which was shortly after, he went off home and his mum must have phoned up saying, you know, 'My son's been attacked by a teacher and had snow shoved down his back' and so on. It got so exaggerated and blown out of all proportion that er . . .

R   She didn't come in the end. I mean it was sort of . . . the head sort of took the phone call and I think he sort of smoothed things over and came and asked me what happened, you know, and I told him, and er it sort of got laughed off in the end

E   but er it shows how things can get so, you know, built up out of nothing really. You know, he probably wasn't the best of kids to do that with. A lot of others it wouldn't have mattered in the slightest.

If the focus of the analysis is on the Evaluation then the teacher's basic reason for telling this story is the explanatory comment, 'Things can get built up out of nothing', meaning that when teachers have problems with parents a common cause of difficulty is that parents exaggerate minor problems. This is a perspective shared by many teachers. However, a more detailed analysis may reveal further cultural perspectives. The narrative can be analyzed as cycles of smaller Orientations — Complications — Resolutions, followed by the final Evaluation. The narrative can then be seen as a series of episodes.

Episode I

O   teacher plans writing, pupils will listen to crunching snow, take it from there

C   teacher anticipates problem of children throwing snow

R   resolves problem by issuing threat

Episode 2
>   O   boy throws snowball
>   C   problem: boy is defying teacher
>   'I've got to do something'
>   R   teacher clashes snowball on boy's head

Episode 3
>   O   snow drips down pupil's neck
>   C   problem for boy: he is wet
>   R   boy goes home, complains to mother

Episode 4
>   O   mother phones the school
>   C   problem for head: accusation of assault,
>   mother threatens to come to school
>   R   head smoothed it over, mother does not come

Episode 5
>   O   head asked teacher, 'What happened?'
>   C   problem for teacher: how to explain to head?
>   R   teacher explained — head (and teacher?) laughed it off

*****
>   E   things can get built up out of nothing

Analyzed in this way this narrative can be viewed as a highly symmetrical cycle of episodes, each episode having three parts. The analysis reveals further perspectives: creative writing can start by providing sensory experience but needs no further planning — the teacher 'takes it' from there; teachers' experience can lead them to predict problems, 'I sort of thought, "It's asking for trouble" ', which they can solve in advance; teachers have to preserve their position and control, which includes the need to carry out threats, even those issued unwisely; children can be unpredictable, 'he went off home'; parents can be unpredictable, they can exaggerate — 'My son's been attacked' — and make threats to come and complain; headteachers sometimes have to deal with irate parents, but they protect teachers, 'he sort of smoothed things over'; problem situations can have humorous aspects which relieve tension in teaching, 'it sort of all got laughed off'; it is important to treat children as individuals and to know the appropriate action to take with each one, 'he probably wasn't the best of kids to do that with. A lot of others it wouldn't have mattered in the slightest'.

With a single narrative such perspectives may be dependent on the individual or on the context. However if such perspectives are evident in the narratives of a number of teachers, then this would be evidence that such perspectives could be cultural. If the same kinds of things were said using the same kinds of linguistic expression this would strengthen the case for saying that such narrative analysis offers the opportunity to distil the cultural perspectives of an occupational group. Chapter 6 presents evidence that there is such a commonality revealed by narrative analysis.

Lexical Signalling

Analysis using the Evaluation model can be supplemented with reference to *lexical signalling*. This is a major aspect of Clause Relations Analysis as developed by Winter *et al.* (Hoey, 1983; Jordan, 1984; Hoey and Winter, 1986). They examine the semantic relations between clauses in order to study the information structures of texts in terms of writers' and readers' inferences. Clause relations are often signalled by key words in a text. A number of information structures have been identified which are reducible to Situation — Evaluation or Situation — Problem — Solution — Evaluation. This information structure correlates very well with the narrative structure of the Evaluation model. Lexical signalling also applies to oral texts.

Many texts describe a *Situation* (Labov's Orientation). An aspect of this is a *Problem* (Complicating Action) which requires a response. This yields a result or possible *Solution* (Resolution) which is evaluated positively or negatively before further action is taken — *Evaluation* (also Labov's term).

There is commonly explicit signalling of the text organization (Jordan, 1984, pp. 152–8). The analyst can search for specific signals of Situation, Problem, Solution, and Evaluation. Examples are shown in table 6.

Clearly there is a wide range of such signals. They can belong to many word classes. Some are context dependent, but many, once seen, are obvious surface signals of information structures and clause relations.

Lexical signalling does not provide a complete heuristic since lexical signals are not always present. Without them, and sometimes even when they are present, the semantic interpretation of discourse relations may be different according to personal understanding. However, the narrative analyst who is aware of such signals will use them to identify the structural elements of narratives, including Evaluations. This use of lexical signals is a back-up to the Evaluation model.

Table 6:   Lexical Signals

STRUCTURE	LEXICAL SIGNALS – TYPICAL WORDS
Situation	situation, circumstance, time, place, person, (use of present perfect and past tenses).
Problem	problem, drawback, need, requirement, concern, bad, awkward, risk, hard, difficulty, crisis, change, accident.
Solution	solution, answer, remedy, cope, suggestion, overcome, improvement, iron out, prevent,develop, tackle, treat, help, implement.
Evaluation	success, failure, better, worse, reduce, control, benefit, enable, delighted, excellent, pleased, disappointed, thorough, great, enjoyment, blessing, understand, super, welcome, neat, nice, okay, happy, does wonders, blossom, develop, come on.

Relevance of the Evaluation Model for Teachers' Narratives

There are several reasons why the Evaluation model is relevant to an analysis of teachers' narratives. Labov's methodology overcomes the constraints of the interview situation by using questions which involve speakers cognitively and emotionally. Such questions elicit narratives, though not too explicitly. Secondly, the model shows that oral narratives of personal experience have a clear internal structure. Appreciation of the structure makes isolating a narrative from surrounding talk relatively easy. Teachers' narratives have such a tructure. Thirdly, the model stresses the social functions of narratives. This is important in considering cultural perspectives in teachers' narratives in informal staffroom contexts and in interviews. The social functions are chiefly focussed around the Evaluation. Some social functions will be seen when whole narratives are speech acts: for challenging, refusing, defending, justifying and so on (Labov and Fanshel, 1977; Labov, 1981). Toolan (1988) has suggested that tellers fashion the narrative structure and content around the evaluative point, rather than vice versa. An examination of the Evaluations in teachers' narratives gives attention to the central focus of those narratives.

A further methodological point is that in Narrative, tellers provide both the context and the interpretation. The Orientation section presents necessary and sufficient information for an audience to understand the point. Teachers motivated by narrative processes will provide enough background on the classroom context for a recipient to interpret their narratives. This means there will be sufficient context for a visiting researcher/teacher who is unfamiliar with the teller's school to understand the point. This is important methodologically since a large number of teachers could be interviewed to elicit narratives without the necessity of observing classrooms or of gathering additional background information. Narratives are contextually self-contained. Tellers provide their interpretation. Labov emphasizes how the Abstract and Evaluation show the teller's interpretation of, and attitude towards, what is told. By examining teachers' Evaluations it should be possible to distil their perceptions on the content of their narratives. If narratives on key classroom issues are elicited in a controlled fashion, examination of the Evaluations on particular themes should reveal teachers' perceptions on those issues. If many teachers give common Evaluations, the perceptions must be cultural, at least in part.

Finally, the Evaluation model does not exclude other approaches. It complements conversation analysts' research and Goffman's insights. It can be strengthened by heeding lexical signals. Culture, cognitive processes, literary sophistication can be taken into account. Key concepts from other disciplines can be used to enrich this model for teachers' narratives.

Wolfson (1976) and Polanyi (1985) have developed the Evaluation model examining performance features and cultural aspects respectively. These are now considered.

Interviews and Narrative Performance

It has been suggested by Wolfson (1976, p. 206; 1982, p. 62) that narratives elicited in interviews lack performance features. They are essentially summaries. If this is the case, interview narratives would be mere shadows of fully performed conversational narratives. To appreciate this argument it is necessary to look briefly at the nature of research interviews.

In the social situation of an interview there are assymmetrical rights to talk (Silverman, 1973; Kress and Fowler, 1983; Walker, 1985). The interviewer has the unilateral right to ask questions, the respondent has the obligation to provide answers. It is the interviewer who determines, initiates, sequences and closes topics. The interview is a specific social situation in which there is necessarily some distortion from objective truth. Past recollections are not so much reports as selectively modified recollections fitted to a current view which a respondent is willing to share (Dean and Whyte, 1975). Information in interviews is negotiated, not only through question and answer, but also through trust and rapport (Briggs, 1986, p. 3; Denscombe, 1983, p. 115).

The interview produces formal speech in the sense that speakers pay attention to how they speak. Labov (1971) called this the 'observer's paradox' (p. 461), the question of how to observe how people talk when they are not being observed. His solution is to elicit narratives, assuming that the emotional involvement of narration implies a more informal style.

Wolfson (1976) put forward several important arguments to modify this. One can tell a narrative in either a formal or informal style, depending on the situation. People know the rules of speaking which are appropriate for interviews as speech events. There are no absolute entities such as natural or casual speech. If speech is appropriate to the situation and the goal, then it is natural, whether it takes place in an interview or not (*ibid*, p. 202). The interview is thus a natural speech event with its own appropriate natural speech. She concludes that narratives elicited in interviews will be different from narratives which occur in other contexts. If confirmed, this could be a crucial limitation in using research interviews to elicit teachers' narratives.

Wolfson distinguishes between narratives elicited in interviews and spontaneous narratives, told in free conversation (*ibid*, p. 192). She makes this distinction on the basis of analysing 150 taped narratives occurring in interviews and 400 taped narratives occurring in a variety of spontaneous situations. She claims that interview narratives are usually in the form of a summary, short and to the point. Respondents know they are answering questions and so details in such narratives are directed to the question. These narratives must be characterized as *answers*. Conversational narratives, in contrast, are more detailed and are *performed*. Speakers choose their own topics, elaborated in their own time. They are not answering questions with narratives.

Conversational narratives are performed, Wolfson hypothesizes (1982, p. 77), when norms for evaluative interpretation are presumed to be shared. Then the point of view that the narrative expresses can be better understood and appreciated by the audience.

Performed narratives have the features (Wolfson, 1976, p. 206) of the historical present tense, sound effects, iteration, present deixis, detailed blow-by-blow accounts of the action. Performance is more likely if the topic is appropriate to the audience, participants have shared background interests and reciprocal relationships, and therefore, (this is crucial to the present argument,) shared norms for evaluation (*ibid*, p. 207). Recent events are more likely to be performed, as are narratives where the central figure is the narrator.

Implications of Wolfson's Work

Two points are important here in relation to teachers' narratives. First, spontaneous narratives are often told in conversation in response to questions and are triggered off by previous spontaneous narratives. There are examples of this in the Headteachers' Conference tape referred to in chapter 1. This is hardly surprising, given the obviously shared norms among primary headteachers, but the narratives are, as in interview situations, naturally tied to the context of previous utterances. If they were not, they would be heard as irrelevant. In that tape of headteachers, it is clear that such 'cued' narratives are certainly perceived by participants as being relevant, judging by the appreciative comments and sympathetic responses to each narrative.

Secondly, in the narratives collected in interviews in the research reported in chapter 6, there are many examples of performance features including the conversational historic present, extensive use of direct speech with use of intonation patterns, pitch range, vocal effects, including whispering, to imitate children, present deixis, sound effects, iteration, detailed blow-by-blow accounts of the action, clear uses of emotional aspects of recounting and suspense. There are also many gestures and non-verbal features which the researcher recalls, but which were obviously not recorded. This list demonstrates that here the teachers performed their narratives in the interview situation. Perhaps this is natural since primary teachers often tell stories to children and are practised raconteurs.

Since the teachers performed the narratives in the interviews, there must have been reasons for this exception to Wolfson's finding. The obvious reason lies in the interview situation (in teachers' own classrooms or staffroom) and in the relations between participants (all teachers — the researcher was a primary teacher too), speaking on topics of concern to teachers. It can be concluded that there were shared norms for evaluation. The interview may have been regarded as an expressive medium, which would have emphasized the performance factor (Denscombe, 1983, p. 111).

Linking what Wolfson says about performance to Goffman's comments on animating and performing a strip of past experience leads to two implications for teachers' narratives. First, if teachers' narratives in interviews bear the signs of performance then those narratives are very close to narratives which occur in informal conversation. To that extent they are representative of normal teacher-to-teacher talk and not artefacts of the interview situation. Second, through performance teachers are presenting their professional selves, animating and performing strips of past experience, reliving the experience. This implies a degree of closeness of the narrative, through recall and reconstruction, to the original events. To that extent the data here seem to be a genuine representation of what occurred (but see chapter 3).

The Evaluation Model and Culture

The work of Polanyi has extended the Evaluation model of narrative towards cultural analysis.

Polanyi (1985) defines the term 'narrative' as a kind of discourse in which a precise time line is established through the telling, made up of discrete moments at which events take place. This definition is broader than Labov's since it permits a reordering of past events (flashbacks, flashforwards) in the telling. However, her term 'narrative' is quite general and it includes plans for the future, commentary, wished-for unrealized occurrences, generic descriptions, reports and stories. A 'story' concerns specific events which occurred at specific times in the past relative to the time of narration (1982b, p. 511). Her use of story corresponds to the use of 'narrative' here, but the term 'narrative' will be used, avoiding the fictional overtones of 'story'.

Following Labov, Polanyi (1979) sees a narrative as having three types of information structures (p. 209). These are the *event* structure (Labov's narrative clauses), *durative-descriptive* information (free clauses used for Orientation, non-instantaneous happenings) and the *evaluation* structure. She stresses that all three structures are 'mutually contextualizing', but it is the 'evaluative metastructure' which picks out the vital aspects of the other two structures to indicate what the speaker believes important to understand the narrative. In this sense the evaluation structure is the most important part of a narrative.

Polanyi believes oral narratives of personal experience illustrate core concepts of culture and that narratives are sources of insight into those concepts. The point of a narrative must be 'culturally salient material generally agreed upon by members of the producer's culture to be self-evidently and importantly true' (*ibid*, p. 207). Events in narratives must be newsworthy, but the point does not have to be, and generally is not. Narratives are built around culturally salient material. They are cultural texts available for analysis.

A method is set up (1979, 1985) to abstract out the culturally salient material. Working with American narratives Polanyi paraphrases each narrative by giving close attention to information foregrounded in the telling by evaluation. The paraphrase is then expanded to show culturally salient American values and beliefs by asking what is interesting or worthy of narration. The expansions are then distilled and organized into a structured list of cultural concepts, an abstract 'grammar' of cultural constructs (1985). This is 'a methodology for identifying and investigating beliefs about the world held by members of a particular culture' (1979, p. 213).

Such a method seems unworkable with a large number of narratives. It would be extraordinarily time consuming to paraphrase, expand and distil each narrative in the manner suggested. However, there seems to be no reason in principle why one should not move directly from a collection of Evaluations to statements about the cultural constructs which they embody.

Implications of Polanyi's Work for an Analysis of Teachers' Narratives

Seeing narratives as cultural texts and using Evaluations in the analysis of culturally salient material is important to the study of teachers' narratives. It gives support to the notion of analyzing the Evaluations in teachers' narratives in order to study teachers' culture, beliefs, perceptions and attitudes. Essentially Polanyi's work suggests taking the Evaluation structures of teachers' narratives, asking what is of interest to tellers about them and putting together many such statements of culturally salient material into a list of teachers' cultural constructs. The paraphrase and expansion stages might be curtailed.

This assumes, of course, that teachers are members of a definable cultural group and that their narratives somehow reflect this. Polanyi (1979, p. 213) points out that inevitably statements of cultural presuppositions look simplistic or self-evident to those who belong to that culture. Cultural statements resulting from an analysis of teachers' Evaluations may therefore look obvious to teachers, but they may be surprising or exotic to those unfamiliar with teaching contexts.

Chapter 4

Psychological Models of Narrative

Introduction

Psychological approaches to narrative focus on the cognitive structures and processes used in the comprehension, recall and summarizing of narratives. It is important to consider these processes in the present context because teachers telling narratives are recalling classroom experiences. Crucial processes of memory are likely to be involved in such narration.

This chapter has four sections. The first outlines the theory of *schemata*, which refers to the collection of models which stress the constructive nature of memory processes and how they may be applied to narratives, invoking expectations and guiding comprehension and recall. The second and third sections examine two main lines of research which attempt to give more detail to story schemata and to predict and explain cognitive processing regularities involved in narration. In the second section Kintsch and Van Dijk's *Macro-structure* model is described. The third section considers the *story-grammar* approach associated with cognitive psychology and those working in the field of artificial intelligence. Since most of the research supporting these models is conducted in experimental situations, the fourth section discusses insights from psychological research into *remembering in natural contexts*. Each of these sections will list insights and implications for teachers' narratives.

Schema Theory: Bartlett and Others

There has been a surge of interest in schema theory since the 1970s. Much of this interest has specifically focussed on the structure and recall of stories, which have proved a testing site for different aspects of the theory. The basic theory of schemata, and the associated terms of frames, scripts, plans and goals will be outlined below. The term 'story' will be frequently used rather than narrative. This follows the usage of those whose work is referred to, and indirectly draws attention to the fact that many of the investigations into schemata use fictional written texts rather than oral narratives of personal experience.

The term 'schema' dates at least from Kant (1787) but in the psychology of memory Bartlett's (1932) work on schemata has become the reference point for subsequent refinements and investigation into narrative comprehension and recall. Bartlett held that recall is 'construction rather than reproduction' (p. 204), an imaginative reconstruction which is hardly ever really exact. 'The past operates as an organized mass rather than as a group of elements each of which retains its specific character' (*ibid*, p. 197). The organizing principle is the schema: 'an active organization of past reactions and of past experiences' which organizes elements of recall into structured wholes.

Bartlett drew attention to key processes of change on the basis of his well-known experiments using the Amerindian 'war of the ghosts' story. In retelling this story, subjects omitted details or condensed parts (*'flattening'*); elaborated or exaggerated other parts (*'sharpening'*); and made passages more compact, coherent and consistent with their own expectations in order to explain incongruous features (*'rationalization'*). All this was in an 'effort after meaning' (*ibid*, p. 55), as subjects used their own schemata as structures of expectation to fill in probable details when recall was partial. Presumably a story schema is derived from repeated exposure to stories and is stable over time and shared within a given culture.

Hunter (1964) summarized subsequent research into long-distance recall of stories and events involving the recallers' emotional attitude. He concluded that recall was conspicuously inferential and constructive in character. 'The very best we would expect of the retelling is that it should give the main characteristics of the story in words which are largely the person's own rather than those of the original' (p. 154). Narratives include 'allegedly direct quotations' (*ibid*, p. 160), but in large chunks of narrated dialogue it cannot be assumed that narrated words are what was said. It is more likely that the teller is using a schema to fill in plausible detail with the kind of thing that is typically said on such occasions or what the teller now thinks a person should or would have said. Tellers are generally unaware of this large role played by their own interpretation, especially in narratives of personal experience.

This work has been criticized by Baddeley (1976) for its artificial methodology. Schema theory is considered too vague and complex to be testable (p. 13). Nevertheless, Baddeley confirms that long-term memory strongly abstracts. Memory load is minimized by stripping away inessential details. Material is encoded in terms of existing schemata. Only sufficient detail of the original event or story is kept to allow a reconstruction on recall. What appears to be a direct record of personal experience is actually a reconstruction based on an abstraction (*ibid*, p. 318). Most recent work on narrative in memory takes the basic position that there are *narrative schemata*, 'the knowledge structures that people use during the comprehension and encoding of simple narrative stories' (Yekovich and Thorndyke, 1981, p. 454).

The general picture of memory for events, and narratives recalling them, is that the process of remembering is constructive, abstractive and integrative (Gomulicki, 1956; Cofer, 1973). Using less exotic materials than Bartlett, and shorter lapses of time, Gomulicki found 56 per cent of narratives were retold verbatim, while 33 per cent of the original material was omitted, 12 per cent involved word changes and 6 per cent was added by the teller. Such a high percentage of verbatim material is very unlikely in long-term recall of narratives. Long-term memory is generally held to be basically semantic — memory for meaning is preserved over time whereas memory for wording or the form of sentences is not (Cofer, 1973; Kintsch, 1974). One exception to this is that there may be excellent verbatim retention of statements in dialogues that have high interactional content (Keenan *et al.*, 1982).

There are five properties of schemata commonly held by schema theorists (Thorndyke, 1984, p. 173). First, a schema represents a prototypical abstraction of the concept it represents, encoding constituent properties that define a typical instance of its referent. Then schemata are hierarchically organized in memory, according to different degrees of specificity. Thirdly, the properties that characterize a schema are represented as variables or slots that can be filled whenever the schema is used to organize information. This means, fourthly, that schemata are used predictively, guiding the interpretation of incoming information, supporting inferences and matching input to expectations. Where expected information does not appear it may be filled in by default. Lastly, schemata are formed by induction from numerous previous experiences.

There have been a number of recent attempts to narrow down the schema concept in specific ways. These attempts have been couched in terms of metaphors: *frames, scripts, plans* and *goals*. Reference to these concepts is frequently made in work on narratives in memory. All of them involve the notion that tellers and hearers have prior experience, organized knowledge and expectations about the world and likely events.

Such structures of expectation make interpretation possible. In the process of interpreting, these concepts reflect back on perception of events to justify that interpretation (Tannen, 1979, p. 144). These metaphors will now be discussed.

Frames

Minsky (1975) suggested that a frame was 'a data structure for representing a stereotyped situation' (p. 212). Hearing a narrative, a person will engage in a process of selecting a previously remembered frame from among a variety of hierarchies of frames and fit the narrative into it (cf. Goffman's sociological frames). Schemas can be represented as frames having slots which can be filled in with appropriate values or information. If specific information is not given for a slot it may be filled in by default as the hearer selects the most commonly expected value. Often such default values are taken for granted. A frame is a rather static representation of knowledge, whereas a script is somewhat more dynamic. Frames are included in Kintsch and van Dijk's macrostructure model of narrative (see below).

Scripts

Scripts are knowledge structures which describe routine events, 'predetermined sequences of actions that define a situation' (Schank, 1975, p. 264). Examples of these stereotyped event sequences are 'ordering food in a restaurant' or 'starting the day at school'. A written out script would list the default values for actions which would be expected to occur in such situations and which therefore do not need to be mentioned. A script is said to be useful because it fills in the blanks in our understanding. Scripts are 'glorified inference techniques' (Schank, 1976, p. 184). Schank views narratives as being sequences of causal links. One problem in understanding a narrative is establishing a causal chain that connects it into a related whole. If a common sequence is involved a script helps teller and hearer because a script is 'a giant causal chain of conceptualizations that have been known to occur in that order many times before (*ibid*, p. 180)'. It can be hypothesized that narrators will script events in a certain way not because they were known to have occurred as such but because that is the typical chain of events in similar situations. In recall, parts of a script which were not mentioned originally tend to be mentioned in later reproduction (Bower *et al.*, 1979). Script actions are recalled in temporal sequence even when presented in a scrambled order. Scripts are said to be linked in memory as sets. When some of the actions are accessed, so are the others. Like frames, scripts are hierarchically ordered. Unlike frames, they are also temporally sequenced (Abbott *et al.*, 1985).

Plans and Goals

Researchers using schema theory have suggested that it is impossible to understand narratives without taking into account the goals, plans and intentions of the characters. This dimension is missing in the Evaluation model. Plans are global patterns of events and states leading up to an intended goal (de Beaugrande and Dressler, 1981, p. 90).

Actions in narratives are recalled better than descriptions (Gomulicki, 1956). Recall of goal-directed actions is better than that of non goal-directed actions (Lichtenstein and Brewer, 1980). On this evidence, Lichtenstein and Brewer conclude that recall of narrative prose is largely determined by plan schemata of underlying events. Bower (1976) found that stories with more tightly-knit goal structures were judged more coherent and comprehensible than stories with less tightly-knit ones and the former were recalled better. Goal-relevant deviations from scripts are remembered better than script actions (Bower *et al.*, 1979). Goals and plans are important elements in episodic story grammars (see below) which attempt to include people's motives and intentions in theoretical models.

Further Effects of Schemas

There are three further sets of research findings on the effects of schemas which are widely recognized. These are, first, that stories can be seen as having a hierarchy of propositions, or ideas. The higher the proposition, the more central it is to the story and readers rate it as being more important. Higher propositions are more likely to be remembered on recall and are more likely to be mentioned in a summary. Summaries tend to include only propositions high in the hierarchy (Meyer, 1975; Bower, 1976).

The second finding is that readers can put scrambled stories back into their original order (Kintsch, 1977a). The removal of material which, it is supposed, is necessary to match important schema elements interferes with both story comprehension and recall (Thorndyke, 1977). Stories in which events of different sequences are so interlaced that concurrent schemas must be maintained for each sequence are rearranged on recall so as to separate the schemas (Mandler, 1978). These two main sets of findings, the levels effect and the effect of violating schema order, are widely held to support narrative schema theory. This shows how much prior knowledge is used by narrative audiences. However, de Beaugrande (1980) seems to make an exaggerated claim in stating, 'The effects of schemas as global knowledge patterns applied to stories have been irrefutably demonstrated' (p. 203).

A third type of finding concerns the cultural dimensions of schema theory. Two studies concerning the universality of the narrative schema arrive at opposite conclusions. They illustrate some of the research problems in this area. Kintsch and Greene (1978) suggested that story schemata are culture specific. They found that white North Americans wrote better summaries of European short stories than they could of native Alaskan narratives. They recalled a Grimm's fairy tale much better than an Apache tale. However, since neither Alaskan nor Apache subjects were tested it is possible to conclude that the European short stories were more comprehensible to members of any culture, including Alaskans and Apaches. A second study by Mandler *et al.* (1980) compared Americans and Liberians listening to and recalling four European folktales and one Vai (Liberian) tale. The amount and pattern of recall for both groups was quite similar, leading to the claim of cultural invariance in story recall. However, only the Liberians recalled the stories from both cultures; Americans were not tested with the Vai tale. A further reservation in comparing the studies is that in the first study stories were read, while in the second they were heard. The results seem inconclusive.

Criticisms of Schema Theory

Schema theory and its associated research has received a number of criticisms (Tarpy and Mayer, 1978; Brown and Yule, 1983; Greene, 1986). The first is that key concepts are insufficiently specified — a major difficulty with much cognitive research. Secondly, it is uncertain whether the concepts are set up to account for all representation of knowledge, or only for certain aspects. If only narrative schemas are considered, this becomes easier. Thirdly, there is the difficult question of relevance. Possible associated knowledge proliferates in story understanding: it is difficult to restrict the concepts to *relevant* knowledge only. Fourthly, the research usually quoted uses written material testing subjects (usually psychology undergraduates) in experimental conditions — the relevance to naturally occurring narratives is uncertain, although there have been psychological studies of natural memory which may help here (see below). Finally, the analysis for any of the schema concepts for any particular narrative is extremely complex and detailed (Meyer, 1975), suitable for testing one or two texts on subjects but not for handling a large number of narratives.

Implications for Teachers' Narratives

Schema theory places great importance on the prior knowledge, expectations and inferencing in interpretation which narrative tellers and audiences commonly use. In these terms, a teacher's narrative cannot be thought of as an exact reflection or reproduction of classroom events and actions. On the contrary, schemata will shape and rationalize occurrences according to that teacher's prior knowledge and expectations. Shaping is likely to depend on the teacher's perception of what is typical, offset by what is tellable and newsworthy. An explanation for this balance between typicality and newsworthiness can be seen in terms of frames of static stereotypical situations and scripted action sequences, with slots filled in by variable instances, some of which will be highly individual and tellable. Schema theory is often thought of as comprehension of written narratives and later written recall of them. However, there is no reason in principle why schemata would not influence oral narratives, in comprehension and production. After all, the central function of schemata is that they are involved in the construction of *interpretations* of objects, events and situations. Teachers as tellers encode narratives schematically, employing frames, scripts and plans and other teachers as listeners employ schematic processes in understanding. The fundamental assumption of schema theory is that situations, events or texts can be understood only in terms of the schemata available to the comprehender (Rumelhart, 1977, p. 301). If they do not fit the schemata they are modified until they do fit. A teller of a narrative must have already used a schema in perceiving and remembering the events recalled. It can therefore be hypothesized that teachers will perceive classroom events in terms of relevant schemata; that short and long-term storage of events and experiences in memory will be influenced by or held in schemata; that subsequent recall and encoding in narration of those events are also shaped by schemata. This hypothesis implies that to analyze teachers' narratives, in particular the Evaluations, is, in part, to analyze the cultural schemata employed by their tellers. Schema theory alerts us to the idea that what is not *told* or explicitly mentioned may be equally important to the tellers. It is unsaid, but intended to be understood by default, as part of a frame, script, or plan.

Schema theory relates to the question of the ontological status of teachers' narratives. The problem is to assess the match between what teachers *say* happened (narrative) and the original *event* (reality). If the focus is on teachers' perceptions of their experiences, then schema theory suggests that perceptions through memory processes are reconstructed and shaped via schemata. Since the schemata are based on teachers' previous attitudes, experience and knowledge, it can be suggested that teachers' narratives are heavily influenced by these. If the focus is on cultural perspectives, the original event and the reality-to-narrative match is less important than the idea that narratives reveal teachers' attitudes and experiences. On the assumption that teachers share an occupational culture, and that this culture also shapes schemata, teachers' narratives may reveal crucial aspects of that culture.

The Macro-Structure Model

Kintsch and van Dijk have developed a comprehensive Macro-Structure model of discourse processing from their previous work in semantic memory and text structures (Kintsch, 1977a; van Dijk, 1977a; Kintsch and van Dijk, 1983). They accept the notion of schemata as basic to understanding comprehension and discourse processes and in their detailed and complex model attempt to give it theoretical substance. They argue that without schemata the appropriate reduction and organization of large amounts of information would make storage, organization and retrieval impossible. Their model is set up to account for the processing of all types of texts, written and oral, but has been particularly exemplified by reference to narratives.

Basic Assumptions

As a preliminary step it is worth listing nine basic assumptions behind the model (Kintsch and van Dijk, 1983, pp. 4–11). There are five cognitive assumptions, that: understanding is a *constructive* process; meaning is *actively* interpreted; understanding takes place at the same time as processing input data, not later (*on-line*); understanding activates and uses *presuppositions* in the form of previous experience, beliefs and attitudes, motivations and goals; understanders and producers

Table 7:   The Macrostructure Model of Narrative

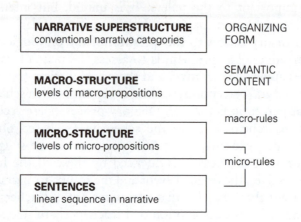

use information from events, the situation or context, presuppositions, and existing schemata flexibly and *strategically*. They also hold four contextual assumptions that: the process of understanding or producing discourse is *functional* in a social context — cognitive and social dimensions interact: discourse has speech act functions (*pragmatics*); speech acts are embedded in participants' interpretation of *interaction*, including their motivations and intentions; there are always constraints on appropriateness to dimensions of the social *situation*.

It is convenient to divide discussion of the Macro-structure Model into three aspects: first, to outline the notion of *macro-structures*, *micro-structures* and the *macro-rules* which link them; second, to analyze the notion of *narrative superstructure*; and third to summarize aspects of *strategic* processing of the model, with some consideration of its psychological reality. This will be followed by a consideration of the relevance of macro-structures and narrative superstructures to the analysis of teachers' narratives.

A diagrammatic overview showing the structural levels of the Kintsch and van Dijk Macro-structure Model is shown in table 7 (after van Dijk, 1977a).

Macro-structures, Micro-structures and Macro-rules

Kintsch and van Dijk analyze utterances and sentences into *propositions*, or elementary units of meaning. Further, they state that propositions must be combined by language users into increasingly higher levels; into fairly specific, lower '*micro*' levels, then into higher, more general '*macro*' levels. This hierarchy of levels is postulated in order to place the semantic representation of a narrative within a framework of cognitive processing.

In the linear sequence of sentences in a narrative as told or heard each sentence contains one or more propositions. These are systematically grouped together into *micro-propositions*, which form the semantic representation of the details of the narrative. A hierarchy of levels of micro-propositions form the *micro-structure* of the narrative, the sequence of propositions underlying the sequence of sentences of the narrative (Kintsch and van Dijk, 1983). Linear sequences of propositions are related to each other by local coherence and cohesion relationships (*ibid*), and to sentences by so-called *micro-rules*.

The semantic representation of the global meaning of a narrative is the *macro-structure* which consists of a hierarchy of levels of *macro-propositions*. The macro-structure is an abstract semantic description of the global content of a narrative and captures the intuitive notions of gist, theme or topic (van Dijk, 1977a; Kintsch, 1977a; Kintsch and van Dijk, 1983). The macro-structure level is concerned with the essence of a narrative and must therefore include the Evaluation. The macro-structure is a coherent whole, not merely a sequence of macro-propositions. In a listener's mind it would be the memory record of hearing a narrative: in a teller's mind it would be the global structure or the central ideas of a narrative. Table 7 is an indication of the macro-structure of these paragraphs.

A macro-structure may be peculiar to a given narrative since it represents narrative content, and narratives differ. Equally, it might be idiosyncratic to a teller or hearer since there are individual interpretations to narratives. However, there are also prototypical aspects to the concept of macro-structure: summaries are based directly on macro-structures; they are used as global retrieval cues in narrative recall; they are schema-based. Comprehending a narrative is essentially filling in slots to a schema outline which is intimately connected to the *macro-structure* (Kintsch and van Dijk, 1983). The larger the number of narratives told on a given topic by a similar group of tellers (such as teachers) the more likely it is that the macro-structures would show a prototypical character.

Macro-structures embody semantic content at an abstract level but they are often directly expressed or implicitly signalled (cf. lexical signalling) by titles, headings, captions, topic sentences, advance organizers, (in writing) and by abstracts, summaries, questions, reminders and all the evaluative devices (in speech).

Macro-structures are held: to define the relative importance of different parts of a narrative in relation to its global coherence; to organize narrative information in memory; to be stored in memory together with some micro-propositional details. They are crucial in the cognitive processing of narratives and provide their overall unity. Kintsch and van Dijk cite a large body of evidence to support the notion of a macro-structure. Kintsch (1977b) concludes 'The pattern of results obtained in these studies generate some confidence that the notion of schema use in macro-structure formation is a sound one.' (p. 61). In this model macro-propositions dominate sequences of micro-propositions but the macro- and micro-structural levels are also dynamically connected by macro-rules (van Dijk, 1977a; Kintsch and van Dijk, 1983). These operate as transformational rules deleting, generalizing and integrating micro-propositions towards a macro-structural level. Their function is to reduce and organize information.

Narrative Superstructures

At the highest level, above a macro-structure is a *narrative superstructure* (van Dijk, 1977a; Kintsch and van Dijk, 1983). Superstructures are organizing principles which are specific to a particular type of discourse. A narrative superstructure determines the overall structure of the narrative text as a kind of macro-syntax for its global meaning. The narrative superstructure provides the global form and organizes the particular semantic macro-structure, the content, while the macro-propositions can be said to fill slots in categories contained in the superstructure. In effect, a narrative superstructure is a special kind of schema, but a conventionalized — not personal — one. Knowledge of such a superstructure is thought to facilitate the generating, remembering and reproducing of macro-structures. The narrative superstructure is non-linguistic but is mapped onto semantic structures.

A narrative superstructure is defined in terms of schematic categories (*ibid*) either using categories similar to the Evaluation model (see chapter 2) or using categories from story grammar (see following section). The first gives a structure in the canonical form of table 8, after van Dijk (1977a). The category of *setting* introduces the characters, time and place and describes the conditions for the events and actions to follow. Each of these sub-categories as state or process descriptions (the form) will be mapped to the macro-structure (the content), assigning specific functions or roles to macro-propositions. The *complication* category is mapped onto macro-propositions interpreting event and action descriptions, the *resolution* category is mapped onto an action description, and so on. Each category dominates a top-level macro-proposition, which

Table 8: *Model of Narrative Superstructure*

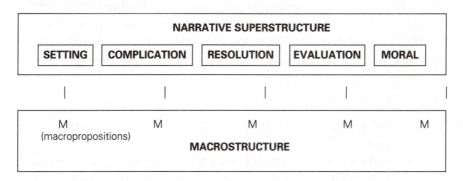

Table 9: *Alternative Model of Narrative Superstructure*

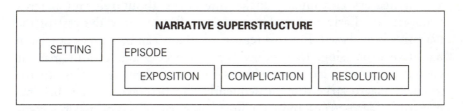

in turn dominates sequences of lower-level macro-propositions. In telling a narrative the categories are filled in with recalled macro-structural content, which in turn is used to retrieve the more detailed microstructural information.

The alternative is to view the Complication and Resolution in terms of Episode structure as in table 9, after Kintsch (1976). The episode category can be recursive to obtain a number of episodes in sequence or hierarchical to get embedded episodes. Mapping to the macro-structure is similar to the other categories.

Kintsch and van Dijk assume that macro-structures: enable comprehension of highly complex information during input, organize the information in memory, and serve as retrieval cues in production. Van Dijk (1977b) claims that 'Experiments have shown that these assumptions are indeed correct' (p. 157). The comprehension, organization and recall of a narrative not only depend on linguistic rules of semantic information reduction (macro-rules), but on the rules and categories determining the global organization of the narrative (the superstructure mapped onto the macro-structure). The narrative structure will determine comprehension, organization in memory, and recall and thus, 'Macrostructure formation in complex discourse is a necessary property of cognitive information processing' (*ibid*, p. 158). This model gives a powerful cognitive processing dimension to the Evaluation model, by equating aspects of the formal structure and semantic content of a narrative with cognitive structures and functions. This aspect will now be considered.

Strategic Processing and Psychological Reality

Kintsch and van Dijk (1983) have developed their original rather structural model towards a more strategic one, building on the basic on-line, strategic and contextual assumptions. The model gives greater emphasis to the formation of a macro-structure and processing strategies. The extraction of narrative macro-structures by hearers is an ongoing process. Far from waiting until the end of the narrative to decide what it was about, hearers continually make inferences about relevant macro-propositions. Early macro-propositions influence how the rest of the narrative is analyzed. For this reason Abstracts can be seen as crucial in narrative processing. In production, first events and actions may be encoded, ignoring later occurrences or fitting them regardless to the invoked macro-structure; subsequently the first events may become narrative macro-structure in a telling, in a cycle of typicality of perception of the expected and subsequent narration of the stereotypical.

There will be a flexible interaction between the inductive, data-driven, bottom-up construction or triggering of a macro-structure on the one hand, and the deductive, conceptually-driven, top-down processing, from macro-structure to incoming data, on the other. In order to know that the discourse is a narrative, the audience will attempt to map the macro-propositions into a narrative superstructure. Once it is presumed to be a narrative, hearers will search for relevant semantic fillings of the narrative superstructural slots.

Apart from the text base (macro-structure), processing also involves the parallel activation and updating of a *situation model* (*ibid*) in episodic memory. This is a cognitive representation of the events, actions, people, and the situation which a text is about. This is continually matched with what the hearer knows about similar situations. Again, this may reinforce perceived typicality. In narrative production tellers first construct a macro-structure as a macro-plan, using elements of general knowledge and of the situation model. The narrative situation model will consist of both the narrative situation and the context of narration, including a model of the hearer and his/her knowledge, motivation and past actions. Secondly, tellers strategically execute the macro-plan, recalling the macro-structure of events and representing their meaning in a narrative structure with all the surface details, including use of stylistic, rhetorical and conversational strategies.

Has this model got psychological reality? The Macro-structure model seems to be based on the premise that *semantic* and *cognitive* structures and processes are closely related and possibly to be somehow equated with each other. Kintsch and van Dijk (1983) seem to be systematically ambiguous about this. Narrative superstructures, they state, are 'not merely linguistic structures or theoretical constructs but have *"cognitive relevance"'*. This is 'a notion with intended vagueness' (p. 239). Whether *some* categories are merely constructs of the theory and others cognitively real, or whether *all* categories and rules of the model are 'known and used as such in processing', can be specified 'in varying degrees of strength' (*ibid*).

Bearing in mind the 1960s psycholinguistic debate over the cognitive status of transformational generative structures and rules, Kintsch and van Dijk are cautious. They do 'not assume that the strategic comprehension of schematic structures necessarily follows the levels or categories of an abstract theory of superstructures' (*ibid*). On the other hand, 'superstructures must be not only in the text, but also *in the reader's or listener's mind*. One must know about conventional schemata before one can use them' (*ibid*, p. 251, my emphasis). They have 'strong theoretical reasons to assume that superstructures must play an important cognitive role' (*ibid*, p. 253). Van Dijk (1988b, p. 52) made a clearer statement: the theory of superstructures is 'not a theory of how language users go about producing or understanding schemata'. Yet this is not the impression one gets from Kintsch and van Dijk (1983). The 'cognitive relevance' of superstructures seems debatable. Ultimately the 'psychological reality' can be examined by considering how well the model explains narratives.

Criticisms of the Macro-Structure Model

Kintsch and van Dijk recognize limitations of the Macro-structure model (*ibid*, p. 121). First, there are possible cultural constraints since only Western European languages have been examined in relation to the model. Also there is surely personal and interactional variation and there may be social constraints in particular settings or with particular participant roles. Aspects of the situation model can take these factors into account. Other criticisms have been raised. The model is said to rely on a single propositional format, which is 'the one major defect' (Johnson-Laird, 1983, p. 386). However, this point seems to be covered by the notion of propositional hierarchies and macro-rules for qualitative

transformations of propositions. It is also charged that there is no procedure for analyzing natural texts (such as conversational narratives)
into propositions and micro- and macro-structures (Brown and Yule,
1983, p. 380; Garnham, 1985, p. 174). This second point is placed in
context by Stubbs (1983): 'no one has yet managed to define propositions in such a way that a definite listing of the constituent propositions
of a text may be drawn up (p. 214). There is reasonable agreement but
not replication. Kintsch and van Dijk show that there is often explicit
signalling of macro-structures.

Implications for Teachers' Narratives

The Macro-structure model gives much greater specification to the nature
and role of narrative schemata. It emphasizes the coherent whole of
narrative macro-structures, and therefore of teachers' narratives. It has
relevance for teachers' narratives through the detailed strategic approach
given to the comprehension, organization in memory and recall of
narratives.

The superstructure-to-macro-structure relationship of narrative is
a more sophisticated form-to-content expression than is usually found
in narrative-sentence relations. The link between the macro-structure
of a narrative and its evaluation seems clear, since the evaluation must
be a high-level proposition in the macro-structure, mapped onto the
Evaluation category in the superstructure. This lends support to the
worthwhileness of investigating teachers' narratives in these terms.

Kintsch and van Dijk's cognitive assumptions are relevant to
teachers' narratives. These assumptions permit a consideration of
teachers' narratives as embodying some element of cognitive reality
showing something of the schematic structures of teachers' memories.
Kintsch and van Dijk's contextual assumptions have already been
considered. Of major importance is the emphasis given to typicality in
the superstructure and in the macro-structures of teachers' narratives
on the same topic, especially if told by a large number of teachers. This
can be linked, through the Macro-structure model, with teachers'
cognitive processing. Another dimension can in this way be added to
research on teachers' narratives.

Story Grammars: Models and Assumptions

In the mid 1970s a number of 'story grammars' were developed which
aroused controversy in cognitive psychology and artificial intelligence.

Table 10:   Basic Categories of an Episodic Story Grammar

EPISODE SYSTEM				
EVENT	GOAL	ATTEMPT	CONSEQUENCE	REACTION

Earlier structural models of narrative analysis, drawing a linguistic analogy between story structure and morphology, had shown that it was possible to break stories down into a small number of minimal recurrent units (Propp, 1968; Todorov, 1977; Greimas, 1983). Story grammarians took this a stage further using techniques of phrase structure analysis and rewrite rules, derived by analogy with generative approaches to syntax. These techniques were used to create sets of rules for segmenting, identifying and manipulating story constituents. The grammar assigns a hierarchical or tree structure to stories.

Story grammars have been sketched out by Rumelhart (1975 and 1977), Thorndyke (1977), Mandler and Johnson (1977), Glenn (1978) and Stein and Glenn (1979). After a setting, the body or plot of a story is composed of Episodes. Something happens to characters causing them to respond or to set up a goal. Their actions or attempts to accomplish the goal result in a Resolution or state of affairs terminating the Episode. Episodes can be linked in sequence or embedded within other Episodes. Details of story grammars and terms differ but all of them parse stories into nodes of information showing how characters solve a problem. A node contains such information as an initiating event, a goal or plan, an attempt to accomplish this goal, and the consequence of doing so. Thus Glenn (1978, p. 230), for example, sees a story as a causal sequence of information, analyzed in terms of six basic categories, a Setting and components of the Episode system, as in table 10. Here the initiating Event causes a response in the main character of the story to bring about a motivating state or internal response which stimulates the character to form a plan sequence (Goal). The Attempt represents the character's overt actions to attain the Goal. The Consequence is the attainment of the Goal, or not, while the Reaction is the character's internal response to the Consequence.

Story grammarians assume that story structures, such as that above, have cognitive processing reality, and are explicitly linked to story schemata (Rumelhart, 1977, p. 301; Thorndyke, 1977; Mandler and Johnson, 1977; Mandler, 1978; Stein and Glenn, 1979; Johnson and Mandler, 1980). Thus Stein and Nezworski (1978) speak of 'isomorphic correspondence between incoming information and underlying cognitive structures' and of a schematic organization of stories 'perhaps reflecting a universal structuring of human memory' (p. 191). Similarly Marshall (1984) states that 'it is a reasonable conclusion' that story grammars 'seem to be descriptive of the way in which narrative information is organized in the mind of both reader and writer' (p. 84). Even those who oppose story grammars as grammars agree that the two main higher level cognitive units in stories are goal-based episodes and thematic plot units (Black, 1984, p. 252).

Results of Research on Story Grammars

Results of research using story grammars generally support schema theory, though there are alternative explanations. Thus texts derived from the grammars are more comprehensible than others not so derived (Thorndyke, 1977). Information higher in the hierarchical structure is better recalled than lower information and is more likely to be included in a summary (Rumelhart, 1977; Thorndyke, 1977). The temporal order of information which is consistent with story grammars is retained better than an order of information which is inconsistent with them (Mandler, 1978; Stein and Nezworski, 1978). Supporters of story grammars take such results as confirmation that the structural relations represented in the grammars are used to understand and remember stories (Mandler and Johnson, 1977; Thorndyke, 1977; Mandler, 1978; Stein and Glenn, 1979). Those who oppose the grammars admit that they have stimulated useful research and thinking into the comprehension and recall of stories (Johnson-Laird, 1983, p. 368).

Criticisms of Story Grammars

Story grammars have generated some controversy (van Dijk, 1980; de Beaugrande, 1982). There seem to be five major criticisms of story grammars. First, they have not been applied to extensive data but only to simple or artificial stories (Brown and Yule, 1983). Second, they are not real grammars in the sense of 'generative' grammar: they do not generate some stories but do generate non-stories (Black and Wilensky, 1979; Garnham, 1988) and they can only be operated intuitively (Brown and Yule, 1983). Third, they emphasize prediction rather than explanation (Thorndyke and Yekovich, 1980), and prescription rather than description (Thorndyke, 1984, p. 188). Fourth, they ignore social interaction and emotive effects (de Beaugrande and Colby, 1979). Finally, they are said to be unnecessary since all that is needed is an understanding of goals and motivations in real life situations or a focus on semantic content only (Black and Wilensky, 1979, p. 227).

Following these criticisms there has been further development and discussion by supporters of story grammars: Johnson and Mandler (1980) proposed a transformational model giving greater economy and flexibility. Mandler (1982) argues that more has been made of the parallel between story and sentence grammars than was intended. A story grammar is only a type of formalism. She adds, clearly 'a story grammar is not a model of mental processing' (p. 434). Story grammars may, however, serve limited heuristic functions to investigate comprehension.

In view of the criticisms various alternatives to story grammars have been proposed, including the theory of 'mental models' (Johnson-Laird, 1983; Garnham, 1983, 1985 and 1988). These are held to contain information about particular situations and refer to what is constructed on the basis of the known, but unlike schemata their structure parallels that of the world rather than that of language. A narrative-specific alternative is the structural-affect theory.

The Structural-Affect Theory

Lichtenstein and Brewer (1980; and Brewer and Lichtenstein, 1981 and 1982; Brewer, 1985) have proposed a structural-affect theory. They attempt to reinterpret the results of story grammar experiments as showing memory for goal-directed events rather than as showing the cognitive structure of narrative schemata. For them, story understanding is only a special case of using event schemata.

They distinguish *events*, a series of events arranged in temporal order of occurrence, from *discourse*, the sequential arrangement of events in a narrative as told. Three types of story structures are distinguished linked with a proposed distinguishing function of stories, the affective function. This function is that stories have a primary function to entertain, thereby getting an affective response. The three structures are surprise, suspense and curiosity.

In the first, *surprise*, the speaker withholds critical information from the beginning, which listeners are unaware of until the end of the story, at which point events are reinterpreted in the light of the surprise. In the *suspense* structure there is an initiating event which could lead to serious good or bad consequences. The listener is concerned about the potential outcome and when informed of it finds the suspense resolved. In the *curiosity* structure the speaker again withholds critical information at the beginning but listeners know this and are curious. When informed later, curiosity is satisfied.

These distinctions seem useful. Brewer and Lichtenstein cite experimental evidence that different discourse patterns produce different types of affective response and that patterns producing affective response were judged by subjects to be stories, while others not producing such a response were not judged to be.

Brewer and Lichtenstein take the category of events and actions to be basic (1981) and understood in terms of underlying event/script/plan schemata. Within this category they put narratives which they define very broadly to include stories, newspaper articles, history texts and directions. An additional level of schema is posited to handle event-discourse relations for narrative.

Stories are characterized by their entertainment function, for which they say, a structural-affect theory is necessary. Others (for example, Stein, 1982) have argued that stories have multiple functions and that one cannot single out one function only for its primacy. The three story structures are linked with affective functions which in turn are related to users' intuitions, mediated by knowledge of the structures and meta-affect, which is the aspect of enjoyment/entertainment. These intuitions and affects are said to be universal (Brewer, 1985) though realized in culturally specific ways.

By recategorizing stories as narratives and actions/events, Brewer and Lichtenstein claim (1982) that story schemata are best interpreted as relating to plan schemata and narrative comprehension. Even here, both story grammars and plan-based theories incorporate goal-directed action sequences as central elements and the structural-affect theory elevates suspense and interest above goal-direction. They present limited evidence to suggest that suspense texts without goal-directed action sequences are considered to be stories by subjects.

Story Grammars and Action Theory

Kintsch and van Dijk take an intermediate position in the story grammar controversy (1983). Their view is that both the specific narrative schemas of the story grammars and the action schemas from the general theory of action are necessary for a complete understanding of narrative.

First, they agree that narratives (Lichtenstein and Brewer's 'stories') are a subset of action discourses. A theory of narrative understanding must include an account of motivations, plans, goals and purposes, which a theory of action provides (van Dijk, 1975 and 1977a). However, while a cognitive account of human action is necessarily very general (not all action discourses are narratives), a specific account is not necessary for either the story grammar or the goal-oriented models.

Second, narratives have specific semantic and pragmatic constraints: what is considered interesting is not inherently part of an action structure (*contra* de Beaugrande and Colby, 1979), but is part of a narrative structure and is culturally variable. Such constraints become culturally conventionalized and normative. Without an interesting action or event, hearers may deny that an account is a narrative, believe it is an unfinished or pointless narrative, or accept it as a narrative from another culture. The narrative category of the macro-structure model theoretically includes these constraints.

Third, knowledge about action is not the same as knowledge about action discourse. Not all aspects of an action feature in a narrative. Only the unknown or interesting is a necessary feature, together with sufficient background to understand it. Since the narrative order of presenting actions is not necessarily identical to the original order in which the actions occurred, they argue that what is important for narrative analysis is not so much a theory of action as a theory of action description.

Implications for Analyzing Teachers' Narratives

The most exciting implication of the story grammar approach is the possibility that a generative approach using rewrite rules and perhaps transformations (Johnson and Mandler, 1980) could be used to account for the narrative structure of the corpus of teachers' narratives. To find a limited number of phrase structures which could describe all and only various types of teachers' narratives would be strong evidence of an underlying structure on schema relating to the typicality of classroom life. However, the story grammar controversy makes it clear that such grammars have conceptual and technical problems with coping with even simple stories, and the 'all and only' criterion would prove too strong to be operable, at the present state of such grammars, on a large corpus of data.

The emphasis on what is interesting will, however, apply to an analysis of teachers' narratives. The entertainment function of teachers' narratives is important, but it is not necessarily the prime or distinctive function. The inclusion of characters' goals and plans could add character-internal dimensions of motivation and response to the Evaluation model. However, a strong element of subjectivity is involved in using such a model on spontaneous oral narratives. Yet it can be assumed that there *is* a plan dimension to the overall organization of a narrative from the teacher's construction of it at the time of telling. 'Plan' may be doubly relevant, then, if subjective.

Remembering in Natural Contexts: Memory Studies

The majority of the psychological studies quoted have been based on the performance of experimental subjects in controlled laboratory tasks, typically reading and recalling narrative texts. In contrast, the teachers in this study were telling oral narratives of personal experience, recalling past events spontaneously in schools. For this reason it is useful to balance the studies referred to earlier by citing some of the few studies of memory in everyday life. It will be seen that these relate very closely to schema theories.

There is plenty of psychological evidence which demonstrates that eyewitness testimony can be 'deplorably unreliable' (Neisser, 1982, p. 93). Memory for real life events is not a copying process. Rather, it is a decision-making process where people see what they want or need to see and actively reconstruct it (Buckhart, 1982). If it is 'replaying a strip' in Goffman's terms (1975), that strip is not that of a tape recorder but of a 'transformation of experience' (Labov, 1972).

Brown and Kulik (1982) saw recollections of the circumstances of hearing significant news as 'flashbulb memories'. Apparently people have vivid images of details of the occasion when, for instance, they heard of President Kennedy's assassination. Neisser (1982) shows how such memories can be wrong and suggests that significance is attached to the experience afterwards through frequent reconsideration, discussion and narration. The photograph-like flashbulb memories can be linked to narrative schemata where personal narrative and historical events become intertwined. 'The notion of narrative structure does more than explain the canonical form of flashbulb memories; it accounts for their very existence' (*ibid*, p. 47).

'Repisodic' Memory

Neisser's study of John Dean's memory for conversations with President Nixon is relevant to narrative schemata and to the role of quotation in narratives. Neisser (1982) compared Dean's legal testimony at the Watergate trial with the White House tapes of the original conversations. Dean had been dubbed 'the human tape recorder' for his apparently

Table 11:   A Framework for Autobiographic Memory

	IMAGINAL	NON-IMAGINAL
SINGLE INSTANCE	personal memories	autobiographical fact
REPEATED INSTANCES	general personal memory	self-schema

impressive memory for dialogue. Neisser concluded that hardly a word of Dean's courtroom account was true, at least, not literally. It was plausible but entirely incorrect. Dean was wrong both as to the words used and their gist. He dramatized. Reconstruction played an exaggerated part in his narrative. Yet at a deeper level he accurately portrayed the real situation, characters and events. Neisser interprets this as 'repisodic memory' (*ibid*, p. 158). What seems to be an episode in narrative actually represents a repetition of a set of typified experiences, distilled into a single account. A repisode is correct in essence even though it is not veridical for any particular occasion.

Brewer's Framework

Repisodic memory can be linked with self-schemata in narrative using Brewer's framework for autobiographical memory (Brewer, 1986). Like Neisser, Brewer draws attention to the difference between single and repeated instances in memory and adds the strong imaginal component of flashbulb memories to give the matrix in table 11 after Brewer (1986).

Personal memories in narrative are recalled as a partial reliving of an episode of the teller's past, typically using strong visual imagery. This would describe a narrative of a unique event. *Autobiographical facts* might be mentioned in the setting of such a narrative. *General personal memories* in narrative typically have generic images of a series of experiences, possibly recalled as a repisode. Brewer indicates that narrators of both personal and general memories may believe strongly that the recalled episodes were experienced. 'This does not mean that they are, in fact, veridical, just that they carry with them a strong belief value' (Brewer, 1986, p. 35).

The *self-schema memory* relates to an assumed cognitive structure which contains generic information about the self. This is derived from past experience and organizes and guides the processing of self-referenced information contained in a teller's social experiences (Marcus, 1977). Brewer (1986) and Barclay (1986) suggest that such self-schemata come to control attention and memory since personal events are recalled in a manner consistent with narrators' self-concepts. There is little research evidence for copy theories of real-life personal memories, but much evidence for reconstructive theory, at least for a partial reconstructive theory. Thus long-term personal and generic narrative memories under strong self-schema pressures are reconstructed and non-veridical. Brewer's taxonomy seems particularly applicable to narratives of personal experience.

To explain the evidence that 'autobiographical memories are not exact' Barclay (1986, p. 95) also draws on the concept of a self-schema. Autobiographical memories are like John Dean's courtroom narrative, paradoxically 'true but inaccurate' (*ibid*, p. 97). His explanation is that self-schemata mediate in personal narratives so that the recollections conform to the existing knowledge of the self. They are true to a teller's self-image. This cognitive account of the self in recalled events complements Goffman's (1969) sociological account of the presentation of self in narrative. Apparently tellers schematically omit, warp or mould events in recall to maintain the integrity and gist of their past life events.

Implications for Teachers' Narratives

These frameworks of remembering in natural contexts are consistent with Schema theories and with the Macro-structure model.

The narrative analyst who is familiar with schema research and studies of natural memory processes recognizes that tellers believe their accounts to be true, yet knows that they cannot be accurate. What is recalled is typical, whether it happened or not (Freeman, Romney and Freeman, 1987). An analyst can resolve this apparent problem with reference to a framework using the concept of self-schema and personal and generic memories. Self-schemata presumably interact with other memories and use frames and scripts for stereotyped situations and actions.

Neisser's (1982) study points up the unlikelihood of verbatim recall of dialogue in teachers' narratives. The concept of repisodic narrative, using general personal memory, again indicates that narration is principled construction. Many teachers' narratives, especially if they are told to illustrate typical situations or events, will conflate recurrent happenings into a repisode. What a teacher tells as having happened once may well be representing repeated experiences. A teacher's narrative possibly tells the analyst more about the typical than the actual event narrated. A teacher's narrative is likely to typicalize the unique.

In summary, the four psychological models of narrative contribute a clear understanding that memory for events in narrative is not exact but is shaped through schemata. Schemata are themselves influenced by repeated experiences, concepts of the self and notions of typicality. The Macro-structure and Story Grammar models suggest that there may be linguistic and cognitive structures of narrative which are composed of a hierarchy of slots filled in by perception and memory processes. If teachers' narratives have many common elements this is because of common perceptions and cognitive processes as much as because of common patterns of events. Studies of natural remembering remind us of the non-veridical nature of narrative recall. They stress the principled construction of narrative, according to self-concepts, repeated events and the way things are typically seen.

Chapter 5

Literary Models of Narrative

Introduction

Within literary theory there is no universally accepted model of narrative, although since the 1970s the theory of narrative has become a central topic in literary study. The continuous shift in the meaning understood by the term 'narrative' in the history of literature, and subsequent description of this, itself illustrates an important point: the tendency for critics and theorists to look for an orderly development of narrative works and narrative theory is evidence of how people use narratives to impose patterns on the past in order to tell a coherent story about it (Martin, 1986). In this way it is suggested that narrative models in literature have developed from Russian formalism through French structuralism towards post-structuralist and reader-oriented theories (Eagleton, 1983; Martin, 1986). Other important recent branches of narrative study include Marxist, feminist and psychoanalytic views.

In the following sections attention will be given to selected concepts of narrative. These are definitions of narrative, views of structural narratology, and some particular aspects of narration including tense, mood and voice. These concepts are derived mainly from structuralist views which attempt to apply by analogy models of sentence grammar from linguistics to literary discourse.

There is an obvious major limitation in transferring insights from literary theory to an analysis of oral narratives of personal experience. Literary theory has primarily focussed on novels and short stories. It is expected that there will be far greater complexity, artistry and imagination in such written works, compared with the spontaneous, oral nonfictional narratives of personal experience. Yet many theorists of literature have paid detailed attention to oral stories in order to understand basic problems of narrative (Todorov, 1969 and 1977; Hendricks, 1973;

Table 12:   *A Minimal Narrative*

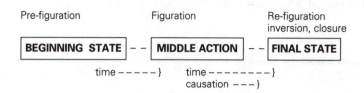

Bremond, 1973; Prince, 1973; Greimas, 1983) and some writers have held that the study of oral narrative reveals fundamental structures and processes of literary genres (Labov and Waletsky, 1967; Toolan, 1988; Maclean, 1988). Conversely, insights from literary theory may illuminate a study of oral narratives.

Definitions of Narrative

In their attempts to define narrative a number of literary theorists have suggested three necessary conditions or criteria. These are *temporality, causation* and *human interest*. The three are seen as combining to form a minimum plot structure. **Plot** is 'the dynamic, sequential element in narrative literature', 'the only indispensable skeleton', the 'most essential' but 'least variable' element of narrative (Scholes and Kellogg, 1966, pp. 207 and 238–9).

Temporality

Temporality is a first necessary condition for a narrative. The notion of plot involves a sequence of events in time. This chronological feature has been stressed since the Aristotelian formulation of plot requiring a beginning, a middle and an end. Other elements of tension, resolution, equilibrium and causation can be included, as in table 12, based on Prince (1973, pp. 19–28), Todorov (1969, p. 74; 1977, p. 111), Chatman (1978, p. 37; 1988, p. 23) and Ricoeur (1984, pp. 52–87). Such a minimal narrative involves three conjoined events: the *beginning state*, a state of equilibrium which pre-figures a change where a character (or the audience listening) envisages what is likely to happen next and plans to intervene to offset the outcome; a *middle action* which sets up tension by a dynamic change or disequilibrium through character action as the events unfurl; and a *final state*, the resolution or outcome which is the *inversion* of the first. The first and second events, and the second and third are linked by conjunctive features of *time*, 'the most fundamental characteristic' of a narrative (Prince, 1973, p. 23).

Causation

Causation is a second necessary condition for narrative. The middle action and final state are linked by causation: the middle action causes the final state. This is 'just as essential a feature as the chronological one' (*ibid*, p. 24). Given the temporal relation, causation is inferred by readers or hearers. What comes after something is heard in narrative as what is caused by that something. This seems to annul E.M. Forster's well-known distinction (1927) between *story*, which orders events temporally, and *plot* which orders events causally as well as temporally.

There are larger patterns: different scholars working in the field emphasize different aspects of these. The three events or states can be seen as alternating with dynamic actions or changes (Todorov, 1969 and 1977). Temporality and causation can be seen as working together as a whole, so that a narrative finishes in resolution of tension (Chatman, 1978 and 1988; Prince, 1973). Temporal succession of events may be a sufficient minimum criterion for a narrative since causality can be projected onto it and some events, intuitively recognized as narratives, would be excluded by causality (Rimmon-Kenan, 1983). However, the consensus is that narrative is not simply a succession of recounted events, but an interesting intelligible whole, where events are connected by time and causation. Plot transforms events into a story (Ricoeur, 1981). At the final state, the audience refigure what led to the outcome. The earliest events are reconnected to take on new meaning; they act as causes only because of the later events. Narrative thus involves 'retrodiction' (Martin, 1986, p. 74).

Human Interest

A third defining feature of narrative is *human interest*, which determines whether the events and causes fit together in a plot with a beginning and an end (Martin, 1986). Without human interest, then there is no narrative, according to Bremond (1966) and Prince (1973). This defining feature seems open to considerably more relative interpretation than the two previous features: what interests one person may not interest another.

Literary Narrative and Linguistic Analogies

These three criteria of narrative are important in structuralist models of narrative. Such models examine narratives in order to find common elements which are transferrable to non-literary media (for example, film, or spoken narrative) and have become the basis of narrative research in studies of popular culture. Proponents of these models use the term 'narratology' to suggest that narrative theory and analysis is an autonomous discipline which can formulate a 'grammar' or 'syntax' of narrative (Todorov, 1967; Prince, 1973; Chatman, 1978). Throughout much of their writing there runs a fundamental analogy between structural (and later, generative) linguistics and the study of literature. The exact nature of this analogy is problematic. It is not clear how literary theorists are using linguistics, whether as a source of metaphors; as a source of methods, analytical techniques and rule systems; as a model, or heuristic device; or as part of a homology between literature and linguistics where the literary work is investigated as a semiotic system (Culler, 1975, pp. 96–109). In one or other of these ways, narratives are treated in terms of sentence grammar. However, it can be argued from a discourse point of view that a text, such as a narrative, is not simply a sentence writ large nor an analogy of a sentence. Texts have their own structure (McCarthy, 1991; Hatch, 1992) and, of course, the initial impetus for narratology was precisely to see narratives as having their own global structure.

Propp's (1968, written in 1928) pioneering study of the plot structure of Russian folktales showed that they had only thirty-one 'functions' or significant actions, which if selected for a particular tale, appear in invariant order. Such functions, together with seven 'spheres of action', or roles, make up the basic units of narration. Essentially these units are seen as *relations* between elements rather than as elements themselves. This valuable insight has inspired later structuralist research into narratives.

Five Traits

Subsequent analysts followed this basic structural approach to narrative. Although there are differences in conceptions and terms relating to narrative units, levels, and rules or constraints on sequence and combination, fundamental common traits can be seen in the work of Bremond (1966 and 1973), Todorov (1969 and 1977), Greimas (1971 and 1983), Barthes (1980) and, perhaps, Levi-Strauss (1968). These traits can be outlined under the five headings of autonomy; story and discourse; narrative deep and surface levels; concepts of actants and function-types; and sequences. These will be briefly examined in turn.

First, narratology is considered to be an *autonomous* discipline. Within this study, an effort is made to define narrative as a specific autonomous level in the semantic organization of texts with its own rules and invariant patterns. As such, narrative (the abstraction from *a* or *some* narratives) can be seen as grammar. This utilizes the concept of grammar, as Greimas (1971) says, 'in its most general and non-metaphorical sense, understanding such a grammar to consist in a limited number of principles of structural organization of narrative units, complete with rules for the combination and functioning of these units, leading to the production of narrative object' (p. 794). Others, such as Barthes, see narrative grammar more clearly in terms of the syntax of a sentence: 'Structurally, narrative shares the characteristics of the sentence without ever being reducible to the simple sum of its sentences: a narrative is a long sentence...' (1980, p. 247). Like Greimas (1983) and Todorov (1969), Barthes exemplifies this with narrative categories corresponding to subject, predicate and verb categories. 'Nor does the homology suggested here have merely a heuristic value: it implies an identity between language and literature' (*ibid*, p. 247).

Second, is the generally recognized distinction between *story* and *discourse*. In Chatman's terms, 'story' means 'the content or chain of events (actions, happenings), plus what may be called the existents (characters, items of setting)', while 'discourse' is 'the expression, the means by which the content is communicated' (1975, p. 295; 1978, p. 19). This distinction corresponds to 'fabula', the pre-narrative events as they occurred, and 'sjuzhet', the plot or narrative as told. This distinction has been used as the basis for commentary on focalization and time (see below).

Third, this is linked with the concept of 'deep' and 'surface' structure. This is derived from linguistics to give the notion of *surface narrative structures*, the actual string of words or text manifested, and *deep narrative structures*, an abstract level of narrative from which the surface text is generated using selections of rules and units corresponding to a generative sentence grammar (Greimas, 1971, p. 797). In some researchers' formulations, 'story' is a chronologically-ordered deep structure (Toolan, 1988, pp. 12–13). In others' views, it is a surface structure which can be paraphrased as labels or propositions (Rimmon-Kenan, 1983, pp. 13–20), but still analyzed for temporality and causality. The deep structure, quite unlike Kintsch and van Dijk's (1983) macro-structure, is based on static logical binary relations (see below)

Table 13: *An Actantial Model of Narrative*

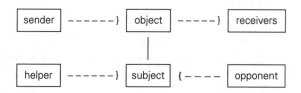

which are said to contain not only universal structures of narrative, but structures of thinking (Greimas, 1970, pp. 160–4) or of behaviour (Bremond, 1973, p. 221). These views echo the debate about the cognitive status of story grammars (chapter 3).

Fourth, is the attempt to set up the specific deep-level concepts of actants and function-types. The 'actantial' model proposed by Greimas (1971) reduces Propp's roles assumed by characters in narratives to a smaller more manageable number. They are regularized into three sets of binary oppositions of *actants*. These are abstract classes of universal roles in stories. They are generated and defined in the deep structure, which correspond to actors: recognizable individual characters at the surface level. One actant can be manifested by several actors or conversely one actor might realize several actants at different points in a narrative.

Greimas' model shows structural relations between actants as in table 13 (after Culler, 1975, p. 233). A narrative cannot be a signifying whole, in this account, unless it can be grasped in this sort of actantial structure. Hawkes (1977, p. 92) gives the example of the Quest for the Holy Grail, where the roles in the story can be related to table 13. According to Hawkes, the Subject is the Hero, the Object is the Holy Grail, the Sender is God, the Receiver is Man. The Sender and Object are more typically abstract than concrete in many narratives, for example, they may be the pursuit of happiness or knowledge (Toolan, 1988). A parallel correspondence is found between surface-level functions and deep-level *function-types* (Grosse, 1978, p. 163), again using a reduced list from Propp's functions.

Fifth, narratologists paid attention to **sequences, combinations** and **hierarchies** of narrative units. For instance, Bremond's (1966) triadic sequences of choices are combined into higher levels of complex sequences by enchainment, embedding and joining (Rimmon-Kenan, 1983, pp. 22–7) giving micro-and macro-sequences. Todorov (1977) and Barthes (1980) suggest hierarchies of levels of different types of units with possible transformational rules relating various levels. Clearly this is modelled on transformational generative grammar and is not unlike the macro-structure model.

In conclusion, narratologists give less attention to content and pay rather more attention to a highly reduced formal system of structural relationships of narrative. Their work emphasizes the organization of narrative as a whole, beyond a linear model. Yet, some of the deeper levels are abstract, atemporal and static, which avoids consideration of a dynamic unfolding of tensions in narrative.

Applying the Actantial Model

An application of the actantial model can be made to teachers' narratives. First, some examples of teachers' narratives about awkward parents are given.

N6   I picked up one child, I separated two children, I think it was in my first year here, separated two children from fighting and they were really nasty. It was hair-pulling, and I picked up one, who was almost hysterical and I had to carry him across the playground into the classroom, and let the other one go home and within ten minutes father was up — this was about a quarter past four — 'Oh, I'm going down the Education about you, mate', 'Down the Education' is the usual one we get (i.e. down to the County Education Office). I was rather new in school and rather, sort of, new in this school and rather concerned about my image and I phoned the headmaster who had already gone home, and he came back and basically said that what I had done was right. Dad was annoyed that I had carried the child. I had 'manhandled' him. I had 'picked him up by his arm and swung him round his neck', according to the parents.

N7   I had a little girl in my class, it's quite a while ago now, she ... I came into the classroom and caught her kicking somebody else so I asked her how she would feel if somebody had kicked her, which I thought was a fair enough statement and it was at the beginning of playtime so I said, 'Right, you can wait till the end of playtime ... I'm not wasting my playtime sorting you out when you've been in trouble, so you can stand by my desk.' I came back after playtime and she'd run home — didn't want to come back to school and she'd probably told her mother that Miss was going to kick her and I thought, 'Oh, no!' So her mother came up at a quarter to four the following day and had a go at me, with the rest of the children in the classroom, so of course I just said, 'Well if you're not prepared to accept my word and you want to believe your daughter and ...' you know, 'you don't want to ...', you know, I said, 'She's obviously misunderstood what I've said. I said, "How would you feel if somebody kicked you", not "if I kicked you"', I said 'and she's panicked. She's thought I was going to kick her and she's gone home.' I say, 'And if you're not satisfied with what I'm telling you, you'd better go and see the headmaster.' No, she wouldn't go and see the headmaster. I say, 'Well, I can't give you any more of my time. If **you** won't go and see the headmaster, **I'm** going to see him.' So I went storming up to the office, you see, by this time I was shaking, I was so cross, and she's threatened to report me to the Education Office, the lot! Of course, nothing like this had happened to me before. It was the first time that it had ever happened but I was absolutely petrified, and I went up and the head calmed me down and sent me back off home and had a word with the mum and calmed her down and I've heard nothing from it since. But I was a nervous wreck when I got up to the head's office. I was shaking like a leaf. I was absolutely petrified because the school I was at before I came here was nothing like this school. I was all on first name terms with the parents and to have a parent come and accuse me of doing something like this, I thought, 'Ooooh.' So I was a bit panic-stricken, to say the least, this parent coming and saying that I was going to hit her child.

These and other teachers' narratives of awkward parents can be analyzed for semantic roles using Proppian functions or actantial models, as in table 13. The parent can be thought of as the Initiator or Opponent, from the teacher's perspective — not, of course, all parents, but the minority in narratives who are seen as awkward. The teacher portrays herself as a victim, an Undergoer or Subject — not, of course, always; only in this particular type of narrative. The headteacher, who supports and shields the teacher, is a Prop or Helper while the child, in this kind of narrative, is an Object. These roles, seen in a number of teachers' narratives of awkward parents, constitute a cultural description of problem parent situations. Not all parents, or teachers, are involved in such situations. The model has a measure of explanatory power for this kind of teacher narrative.

Table 14: A Semiotic Square

x	y
both x and y	neither x nor y

Table 15: A Semiotic Square for Parent–Teacher Relations

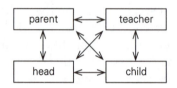

In another abstraction of narrative structure, Greimas suggests that the actants or functions in a given narrative can be invested with further meaning by being inscribed in a 'Semiotic Square' based on logical relations which go beyond a binary model (Schleifer, 1987, pp. 93–126). An abstract example of a semiotic square is given in table 14, following Schleifer (1987). In such a square, horizontal relations are contraries, diagonals are contradictories and verticals are complementary, showing key oppositions. In table 14, x and y are opposites. The item in the lower left square has qualities of both x and y, while the item in the lower right square has qualities of neither. A semiotic square gives the deeper meaning of narrative as equations of meaning, rather than of action. Such an abstraction of underlying values could be made from teachers' narratives, again following up an analysis of N6 and N7 and other narratives about awkward parents. The roles in these narratives can be placed in a semiotic square as shown in table 15.

The square expresses the narrative relations in N6 and N7 and other awkward parent stories. Parents and teachers have contrary knowledge of a child, contrary social experience of the child and, on some ways, conflicting interests regarding the child: they both see the child as an individual, but the teacher must also always see the child as a member of a class, considering discipline, safety, and collective learning. Both parents and teachers want the best for the child but parents often do not see the context of the whole class, so, as told in narratives, teachers often have to point out the class context and their responsibility for many children, not only this parent's child. The Child is neither Parent nor Teacher but is the focus of attention of both, although in different ways. Where problems in parent–teacher relationships arise, the headteacher, or Head, combines aspects of both Parent and Teacher, whilst remaining identified with neither. The Head, in narratives, is said to listen to both, and to be fair to both in a mediating role. Much of the Head's job is seen as involving home–school liaison, of course. However, in this group of narratives the Head is portrayed as shielding and supporting the Teacher. This role is further illustrated by these extracts from the narratives of two headteachers:

N8   Usually I say I'll have a word with both parties in the morning and try to sort it out. I don't think you can accept the word of the one who is complaining.

N9   Let them (parents) understand that you are prepared to listen to them and that they understand you are prepared to be fair. You've got to be fair to your parent and your teacher. I'm the first line of defence. In fact, all things come to me first. The teacher may or may not be involved subsequently, a lot depends on what we discover in conversation.

Further Frameworks of Narratology

Following Genette's work (1980), a number of central categories of narrative analysis have been developed in narratology (Rimmon-Kenan, 1983; Bal, 1983; Berendsen, 1984) which have attained wide currency. Genette (1980, pp. 71–6) adds to the familiar distinction between *story* (*histoire*), the events which occurred, and *discourse* (*récit*), the events as recounted, a third term *narration*, the act or process of narrative production. These terms are systematically related to each other by three categories derived from the grammar of the verb: *tense*, which is concerned with the arrangement and display of events in time; *mood*, under which heading the perspective and distance of the narrator are examined; and *voice*, where kinds of narrators and the ways of representing speech are considered. There are further sub-divisions shown in table 16 (after Genette, 1980).

This framework is set up to analyze literature, especially the novel, but it can be applied to teachers' oral narratives of personal experience or their written biographical accounts.

Table 16:   Genette's Model of Narrative Discourse

TENSE	MOOD	VOICE
order	*focalization*	*narrators*
analepsis	external	intrusiveness
prolepsis	internal	first-person
duration	*distance*	*speech*
summary	diegesis	direct
scene	mimesis	indirect
frequency		
singular		
repeated		
iterative		

Time (Tense)

Time is a basic category of human experience. It is a structuring and structuralist notion involving the perception of events (Rimmon-Kenan, 1983). This is forced into a linear and irreversible form when the events (story) are told in spoken narrative (discourse). The categories of order, duration and frequency are set up to account for differences between event time and narrative time. Under the category of *order*, departures between order of occurrence and order of presentation in narrative are discussed. The major departures, or anachronies, are analepsis and prolepsis. The first describes a flashback or expository return to an earlier period of time, either outside the existing narrative time span or inside it. This usually gives past information about characters or events, filling in omissions resulting from lapses in the teller's memory or through design to change the audience's interpretation of what has been told so far. There is an example of this in N7 where the teacher puts in the information discovered later — that the child said she was not coming back to school and had 'probably' told her mother that her teacher was going to kick her — as necessary for the audience's understanding, but also for dramatic effect. The second aspect of order refers to a flashforward or foreshadowing of an event to be recounted later. This removes the suspense of 'What will happen?', replacing it with 'How will it happen?' Some narrative abstracts have proleptic functions.

    Duration measures the length of story-time against discourse time. Orally, this is the time it takes to tell a sequence of events compared with the time span of the original occurrences. Duration is described as summary and scene. In summary the pace is accelerated by compressing story time into a shorter telling time. In scene, story and discourse are considered to take the same time, commonly in dialogue. Other aspects of duration involve a slow-down, where discourse time exceeds story time, or a pause, where narration continues but the story momentarily stops (Cohan and Shires, 1988). An ellipsis occurs when the narration omits a point in story time. Narrators exploit duration to highlight important events by devoting more telling time to them.

The third category of time is *frequency* of mentions in narrative discourse. An event which occurred once and is mentioned once in a narrative is singular. Other events which also occurred once may be mentioned several times, receiving evaluative emphasis through repetition. An example of this occurs in N7 where the teacher says 'I was shaking', 'I was shaking like a leaf' at different points. Some events occurring many times may be narrated only once (iterative). Genette also considers the pseudo-iterative, where the narrative tells of an event as having happened repeatedly but whose very particularity makes it seem undeniably singular. This would also evaluate an event heavily.

Mood

Under the heading of mood Genette (1980) considers the notion of narrative point of view or perspective through *focalization*, which can include cognitive, emotive and ideological orientation (Rimmon-Kenan, 1983). Focalization is a triadic relationship between the narrating agent, the person recounting a narrative; the focalizer, the subject or character in a narrative who sees; and the focalized, who or what is being seen as object (Cohan and Shires, 1988). Genette (1980) distinguishes external focalization, where the narrative is told by an observer focussing *on* a character, from internal focalization, where the narrative is focussed *through* the consciousness of a character. The focalization can shift from external to internal. It can be fixed, variable or multiple, by shifting between characters. In first person narrative, this distinguishes 'I' the teller, a narrator with a present self, from 'I' then, a character in the narrative at that time with a past self (see chapter 2). Narrators may describe past experiences from either past or present perspectives and the significance of the described events may be viewed by a self who has changed between story time and telling time (Martin, 1986). This suggests a sophisticated 'shift of the I' in narrative which, drawing on Rimmon-Kenan (1983) and Cohan and Shires (1988), can be diagrammed as table 17.

Table 17:   Focalization: Point of View in Narrative

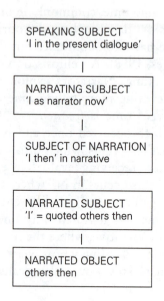

SPEAKING SUBJECT   'I in the present dialogue'
NARRATING SUBJECT   'I as narrator now'
SUBJECT OF NARRATION   'I then' in narrative
NARRATED SUBJECT   'I' = quoted others then
NARRATED OBJECT   others then

Here the **speaking subject** is the present speaker in conversation before telling a narrative. The **narrating subject** is 'I', the speaker recounting a narrative, the person present who experienced these events then. The **subject of narration** is the 'I' of first person narrative at that time, the experiencing self then, who may be different from the narrating subject.

Many narratives will feature other characters, focussing through their perspectives. The teller will often speak for them and speak through them, quoting speech by them as **narrated subjects**. The narrative will also be about other third person characters. These **narrated objects** can in turn become narrated subjects, which assumes, as narrators seem to do, a degree of narratorial omniscience.

A framework like this can be helpful in penetrating the various levels of teachers' narratives, as shown in N7, where the teacher tells the story, in the course of which she quotes herself. However, from the studies on verbal memory about words recalled in narrative and natural speech it is not likely that these are, word for word, the exact words at the time, as chapter 3 showed. The teacher quotes herself talking to the child in one way, talking to the parent in another way and thinking to herself, twice, in a third way. She also quotes herself to the parent as quoting herself addressing the child, in front of the children in the class who were the audience then. The repeated intervening 'you know', said as an aside to the researcher as immediate audience for the narrative, suggests that these are not simply quoted words but the kind of thing one says or typically would say to a parent in this kind of situation when one is a teacher, as both the teller and researcher were. The framework may thus help explicate not only point of view but cultural perspective: ways in which teachers talk about and think about their work, sharing how they see and say things.

Returning to table 6 and Genette's second category of mood, **distance**, this draws on the Platonic terms of diegesis and mimesis. Diegesis, the telling of the narrated events, relates closely to summary whereas mimesis, the showing or direct representation of what occurred, relates to scene. Booth (1987) pointed out that in narrative the idea of showing is illusory. A narrative cannot show or imitate, it can only tell in a detailed, precise manner because language signifies without imitating. However Genette (1980) points out that language can imitate language. Quoted dialogue can be mimetic especially in oral narrative performance. Otherwise, there are only different degrees of diegesis, where the teller is more distant from the told. In teachers' narratives there are frequent performed quotes from children which are mimetic in this way.

Voice

Under the heading of voice, Genette (1980) and Chatman (1978) suggest scales of authorship: real/implied **narrator**, narratee, real/implied audience. Degrees of intrusiveness can range from the impartial description of settings and identification of character, through the more involving temporal summaries and definitions of characters, and reports of characters' speech and thoughts to commentary by the narrator. The high-profile end of this scale includes the teller's interpretation and judgments of events (Rimmon-Kenan). The high-profile end evaluates narratives greatly.

The distinction between direct and indirect **speech** has received much recent attention in literary narrative analysis (Banfield, 1973; Genette, 1980; Dali, 1981; Berendsen, 1984). McHale (quoted in Berendsen, 1984, p. 155) suggests a scale from the diegetic to the mimetic: diegetic summaries, indirect paraphrases, free indirect discourse, direct discourse and free direct discourse. The latter would be pure mimetic dialogue, omitting any verbs of saying (she said/told/ asked . . .), apparently conveying immediacy and accuracy.

Criticisms of Literary Models

There is a large body of critical literature on structural models of narrative analysis (for example, Culler, 1975; Martin, 1986), most obviously from the point of view of post-structuralist, or deconstructive theories (Eagleton, 1983; Selden, 1985). In these, attention has shifted away from the narrative text towards processes of narration and reading, with a reduction in the claim to scientific rigour which had been put forward by the structuralists. A number of criticisms have been put forward. First, there is an over-emphasis on structure and rigour. This is held to be reductionist at the expense of narrative content (Eagleton, 1983; Martin, 1986). Then, there is the question of the relationship, constantly invoked in narratology, between sentence grammar and narrative structure. The criticism is simply that linguistic models of sentence grammar do not apply to narrative discourse. Linguistics, it is said, should be a source of methodological clarity rather than metaphorical vocabulary (Culler, 1975, p. 257). An example of this lack of clarity is the relationship between deep and surface structure in some narrative models, unlike the well-established and widely recognized relationship between these two levels in sentence grammar. There is also the charge that these models of narrative analysis ignore historical development and change (Selden, 1985). Perhaps one reason for this is that the early structural models of narrative were genre-specific, for example dealing with an admittedly restricted set of Russian fairy tales or the stories of Boccaccio. Some of these models also rely heavily on paraphrasing prior to analysis (for example, Todorov, 1969), and this is a further problem since the analyst may be relying on intuitive summaries.

Implications of Literary Models for Analyzing Teachers' Narratives

The obvious caveat about applying literary models to teachers' narratives is the danger of seeing what are usually oral narratives in the first instance in literary terms without appreciating the psychodynamics of orality (Ong, 1982). These models have never been applied to oral narratives of personal experience, although to do so would offer useful insights. Structural narratology reveals that literary narrative is a construct broadly similar to other forms of narrative, and, of course, much of the early structuralists' work was done on folk literature, which was orally transmitted over generations. Instead of positing the dichotomy of written/oral narrative, it may be more useful to see narrative in a continuum. In this case structural models may offer insights and applications at various points along the continuum, including teachers' narratives of several sorts.

There are several aspects of narrative which are emphasized in some structural models which can usefully be taken into account: that a narrative is viewed as a whole, with its own internal structure of mutually related units; that some units of narrative are organized in hierarchical levels (see Macro-Structure model); that some units can be seen as deep level semantic patterns of binary relations or semiotic squares.

Literary structuralists claim that language creates narrative rather than reflecting it. Lodge puts it thus: 'It is not so much man that speaks language as language that speaks man; not so much the writer who writes narrative as narrative that writes the writer' (quoted in Gibson, 1973, p. 94). Such a claim draws attention to the possibility that narrative form may mould the recounting of teachers' experiences in ways inherent to narration as a mode of thought. Certainly there are times when different teachers in different schools independently tell about the same sort of thing in the same sort of way using the same sort of language (Cortazzi, 1991). They may have common experiences and simply use the same language to recount it, or, as some structuralists suggest, it may be that the narrative is telling the teacher. Deep structures and actants tell their own story or mould memories or minds. Teachers are unlikely to be conscious of the above. They are much more likely to focus on the narrative content in teacher-to-teacher talk. Yet it would be important to recognize the formative influence of narrative structure on content where, for example, teachers learn about pupils via colleagues' narration.

As shown in this chapter, there may be abstract recurrent patterns of character (actants) or events (functions) in teachers' narratives on specific topics. These can be formalized in sets of binary relations or in semiotic squares. The framework of story — discourse — narration, with its elaborate classifications of time, perspective, narrators and speech is richer than the Evaluation or Macro-structure model on these points. Analyzing teachers' narratives in terms of order, duration, frequency, focalization, distance and speech could reveal insights into how teachers tell narratives or, more generally, into the process of oral narration of personal experience. It is likely that an analysis taking these aspects into account will show that teachers' narratives are more complex than is at first apparent.

Chapter 6

Anthropological Models of Narrative

Introduction

Anthropologists study narratives in terms of the cultural patterning of customs, beliefs, values, performance and social contexts of narration. Culture can be viewed as symbolic behaviour and patterns of the organization, perception and belief about the world in symbolic terms (Sherzer, 1987). In the first section of this chapter the notion of 'ways of speaking' will be introduced. Later sections consider the structure and function of narratives in different cultures and studies of narrative performance. The extent of narrative studies in anthropology can be gauged from Grimes' comment, made in 1978, that studies of narrative patterns in oral texts had been made in over 100 languages in at least twenty-five countries (p. 123).

Much anthropological research has seen narrative in broad terms to include myths, folktales, legends, reminiscences and jokes (Bascom, 1965). Some reference is made to this broad range of narratives here but more specific attention is given to oral accounts of first hand experiences in different cultures.

Ways of Speaking

Anthropologists and sociolinguists increasingly think of discourse in terms of *'ways of speaking'* (Hymes, 1974) and the 'ethnography of speaking' (Gumperz and Hymes, 1972; Bauman and Sherzer, 1974; Saville-Troike, 1982). As a discourse genre, narrative is seen as a speech event and 'ways of narrating' involve variations according to components of the narrative situation: the participants, setting, purposes of telling, communicative key and cultural norms. Whether a narrative is told, and what kind and how, may therefore depend on who the teller and audience are, what the relationship between them is, where they are, why the narrative is being told, what kind of mood or tone is present and how all of these aspects normally relate to each other for any particular cultural group. The same story can vary if one or more of these aspects of the communicative situation are changed.

With these factors in mind, anthropologists give close attention to cultural ways of telling and the relationship between narrative styles and contexts of narration. These aspects are, of course, related to content. A broad division is made between *referential* and *social* meaning (Hymes, 1977, p. 201). Referential meaning broadly describes the content to which the narrative refers. Social meaning, the social, affective or moral value a narrative may have, is a less obvious aspect of narrative, especially among narrators in a professional group. From this perspective narratives and narrative processes will vary enormously in different cultural groups, because people 'talk differently, about different topics, in different ways, to different people, with different consequences' (Barnlund, 1975, p. 435). Such differences depend on a group consciousness of norms of speaking and the perception of different abilities, rights, rules, roles and status in communicative situations where narration takes place. Different ways of speaking depend in large part on the social perceptions and interpretations of different cultural groups.

Opposite ideas about narrative are found in different cultural groups. Among the Gbeya in central Africa it is believed that no one is a good storyteller (Hymes, 1977, p. 127), whereas among the Limba it is held that anyone is a potential storyteller and it takes no special training to give a good performance of a narrative (Bauman, 1975, p. 299). When she compared the narratives of Greek and American women, told after viewing a film, Tannen (1980) concluded that the Greeks seemed to be 'acute judges' who recounted events and interpreted them, ascribing motives to characters and offering judgments. In contrast, the Americans were 'acute recallers' who gave more detailed, objective reports and showed concern with time reference. While Americans focussed on content, Greeks focussed on interpersonal involvement.

Such variations in ways of speaking are commonly seen as reflections of cultural differences. However, speaking is itself a part of cultural behaviour and it partly shapes and mediates the whole (Hymes, 1977). Language is both cultural, as a form of symbolic organization of the world, and social, since it reflects and expresses group memberships and relationships. 'It is discourse which creates, recreates, modifies, and fine tunes both culture and language' (Sherzer, 1987, p. 296). Narrative, then, is a discourse structure or genre which *reflects* culture. It is a central *medium* of cultural expression, organization and learning. Furthermore, it also *creates* cultural contexts. Staffroom storytelling among teachers is thus a cultural context which comes into being as a story is told and appreciated. This cultural context has its own ways and carries its own meanings, and these may be quite different from the investigatory or analytical ways involved in doing research.

The Structure and Function of Narrative in Different Cultures

There have been numerous anthropological and folkloristic attempts to analyze the structure and function of oral narratives in particular cultures (Colby and Peacock, 1973; Clement and Colby, 1974). Many of these are second or third generation developments of Propp's work (1968/1928), yet this research has not shown cumulative development. Each investigator has tended to invent new terms, units and levels of analysis to develop taxonomic or generative models rather than develop or refine a generally accepted model (Jason and Segal, 1977, p. 4). An example is Colby's model of narrative analysis.

Colby's Model

Colby (1966a, 1966b, 1973a and 1973b) set up a basic unit of plot, which he calls an 'eidon', as part of 'eidochronic' analysis (*eidos*: idea, image; *chronos*: time sequence). Some cultures were shown to have a relatively stable distribution of narrative plot elements, which might, however, differ from the distribution of another culture. He found that an analysis of Eskimo folktales required different units in different sequences, compared to the units and sequences of Russian tales suggested by Propp. He then compared Japanese and Eskimo folktales. Eskimo tales emphasized the personal abilities of individuals, especially physical ones, whereas the Japanese tales showed a concern for the external social situation. This can be interpreted as a reflection of the two different physical and cultural environments. From such evidence Colby (1973b) argues that different types of narrative in a particular culture would each have separate narrative grammars. An acceptance of the cultural diversity of narratives implies that there should be culture-specific narrative grammars. A further implication is that if professionals, such as teachers, are considered to belong to specific cultural groups, then occupation-specific narratives can be expected among them.

Table 18: Longacre's Scheme of Discourse Types

	– projected	+ projected
+ succession	**NARRATIVE** first/third person agent oriented accomplished time chronological	**PROCEDURAL** non-specific person patient oriented projected time chronological
– succession	**EXPOSITORY** no necessary reference subject-matter oriented time not focal logical	**HORTATORY** second person addressee oriented mode, not tIme logical

Colby's framework and complex system of diagramming narrative structures have not been widely taken up in anthropological linguistics. However, others such as those of Longacre (1976) and Grimes (1975) have been more widely used to describe narrative structure and function in a great variety of languages in many cultural groups. Longacre's analysis of narrative structure will be described here and related to narrative structures in a number of cultures.

Longacre's Model

Longacre (1976) distinguishes **Narrative** from three other major types of discourse genre: **Procedural** discourse referring to 'how-to-do-it' texts or talk, **Expository** discourse involving explanations or 'essays', and **Hortatory** discourse referring to persuasive texts or 'sermons'. The differences between these is summarized in table 18 from Longacre (1976, p. 200), where the main distinctions depend on the nature of the succession of utterances, whether chronological or conceptual/logical and how time is projected. In table 18, narrative is differentiated from the other genres by having: chronological linkage, because time sequences are crucial; agent orientation, rather than orientation to 'patient', subject-matter or addressee, i.e. they are predominantly oriented to *who* carries out actions; accomplished or real past time, rather than the projection of time towards the future of prophecy or instruction. Narrative is uttered in the first or third person. Finally, most narratives involve some sort of struggle or plot and have tension — if not, they

Table 19:   Longacre's Model of Narrative Structure

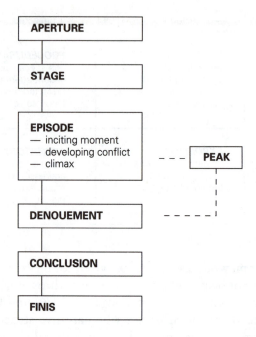

are said to be episodic. In this scheme of different discourse types it is emphasized that narrative is a major mode of oral communication in different cultural groups (Longacre and Levinsohn, 1978, p. 104). The scheme is said to be essentially a scheme of deep structure. The overall surface structure of a narrative, according to Longacre's model, is shown in table 19 (after Longacre, 1976, pp. 199–217; Longacre and Levinsohn, 1978, pp. 104–5).

The *Aperture* is an optional formulaic opening ('I remember the time when . . .'). The *Stage* presents necessary information about time, place, local colour and participants (cf. Labov's Setting). *Episodes* are likely to have an inciting moment which 'gets something going', a developing conflict which intensifies the situation (cf. complication) and a climax which resolves the conflict (cf. resolution). A whole series of episodes may have a *Denouement* or crucial final event which re-solves tension and confrontation. The optional *Conclusion* refers to a narrator's comments or interpretation before an optional *Finis*, or formulaic closing ('And that was that'). Clearly Longacre's framework has much in common with the independently conceived Evaluation model of Labov (see chapter 2). Parallel to the Evaluation of a narrative, Longacre (1976, pp. 217–31) suggests that narrators give marked attention to the main points, or *Peaks*, in a variety of ways which supplement the aspects of Evaluation mentioned by Labov. Peaks are shown by a rhetorical underlining, any kind of special marking or emphasis. This may be by using paraphrase or repetition. It can be carried out by concentrating the narrative characters together, as on a crowded stage. Peaks are also marked by several possible changes allowing that part of the narrative to stand out from the preceding or following parts. Such changes include tense shifts (for example, from past simple to historical present), person shifts (for example, from third to first person), transitions from narration to dialogue or drama (dialogue without formulae of quotation), a change of pace (for example, varying sentence length), and a change of vantage point or orientation, including role reversal (Focalization). All these give a narrative heightened vividness. Further, it is possible to see Episodes organized with reference to one or more Peaks, as pre-peak, post-peak or inter-peak Episodes. A series of Episodes is commonly expected.

Narrative Structure in Different Cultures

This anthropological narrative framework can be illustrated with reference to a number of cultures (Longacre and Levinsohn, 1978; Grimes, 1978; Brewer, 1985). This will show something of the cultural diversity in oral narratives. Examples of opening formulae at the **Aperture** are 'Let us listen' (the Dan language of Liberia), and 'I want to tell you a story' (Hanga in Ghana). Some narrators explain their plans and the purposes of the narrative at this point (Khaling of Nepal, Nafaara of Ghana).

In setting the **Stage**, with regard to time, Godie speakers in the Ivory Coast start the narrative in remote time, switch to proximate time for the main episodes, but will switch back to remote time to emphasize the narrator's personal involvement, or Evaluation. In the Kuna language of Panama, a narrator may jump back and forth from place to place, a practice which a European would find 'illogical' and incomprehensible (Sherzer, 1987, p. 305). In the Jirel language of Nepal, time and place information is always introduced before participants, while in Khaling, also in Nepal, spatial, temporal and character information occur in the Stage invariantly in that order. On the other hand, in Wobe of the Ivory Coast the order of information is time, place, then participants. Narratives in some languages are told in elaborate schemes of spatial reference by establishing a primary location to which secondary locations are systematically related by means of motion verbs (Maxakali of Brazil, Oksapmin of Papua New Guinea). Concerning participants, all characters who will appear at any point are introduced in the Stage in Longudu of Nigeria. Many cultural traditions introduce characters in threes, but in Navajo in North America characters come in fours and in Clackamas in the Pacific Northwest in fives. However, a trio of characters is so common in different cultures that Longacre and Levinsohn (1978) suggest that such a group of three have the abstract roles of Initiator, Undergoer and Prop (cf. the roles suggested by Propp). Different cultures mark the narrator's viewpoint (Focalization) in various ways. It requires a special morphological marking in the verb in Oksapmin, perhaps to evoke sympathy but similar marking cannot be equated with sympathy in Catie, where the viewpoint is that of the villain, with whose deeds the teller does not sympathize.

Turning to the **Episodes,** in Tharu of Nepal and in Nchimburu of Ghana events are invariably told in their order of occurrence, which rules out flashbacks. In Dan of Liberia there is an absence of simultaneity of events in narrative: no two events are recounted as happening at the same time, only sequentially. There are different cultural patterns of linking events: in Kayapo of Brazil an entire paragraph is repeated nearly verbatim as a lead into the next paragraph which describes new events. In Nepalese Kham narrative speakers use two sets of verb endings: one is employed to mark information which hearers will need to understand later information, the other singles out sections of the narrative which are to be responded to directly in the light of foregoing presentation. At the climax of a Kham narrative, hearers are invited to respond as though they were in the situation themselves. This converts action to the present tense and is more common in personal narratives than in other types.

After a **Conclusion,** narrators of Toura narrative in the Ivory Coast give exhortations to their hearers. In Hanga of Ghana and in Mundaruku of Brazil there is always some evaluative commentary, beginning with 'because of all the foregoing . . .' In Nepalese Sherpa narrative, the moral is followed by a summary of events related to the moral, reinforcing the moral connection.

Sometimes parts of a narrative can be used instead of the whole. Among the Ntumu of Cameroon wisdom is distilled into proverbs which are used in tribal jurisprudence: every proverb is the final line of a narrative, but the proverb can be used alone to represent the whole (Sheppherd, 1988, pp. 100–1). Similarly, in many Chinese narratives a final saying or moral of four words is popularly used as a summary or substitute for the narrative in conversation between those familiar with the culture. In Persian this occurs with the poet Saadi's popular literary work of short narratives, the *Golestan*, where couplets serve the same function. In such cases the quoted proverb, moral or verse may be incomprehensible to listeners unfamiliar with the narrative. The quoted extracts are equivalent to Evaluations (see chapter 2), and such cases of the systematic extraction of Evaluations imply a widespread consciousness of the Evaluation function among various cultures.

Narrative Functions in Different Cultures

Such examples show a range of cultural variation in the internal structure and function of narrative. There is also variation in the global function of narratives. Longacre (1976), Labov (1972) and others indicate that narrators take pains to highlight the main point or peak of their narratives with Evaluations and rhetorical underlinings. This does not seem to be universal, however. In Chinese culture 'narrators mention the main point only very briefly and then pass on, while going into great and repeated detail about common experiences in shared time and place' (Zhang and Sang, 1986, p. 368). This may be because of a listener orientation which gives listeners credit for the ability to spot the main point after they have been carefully led to it, or it may be to stress group solidarity in common experience which is a notable feature of Chinese culture (Hsu, 1981).

Preston (1978) suggests four main functions of Cree narratives in Canada. The most important is to define and express basic cultural categories in the sharing of individual experiences. Narratives also share news, provide entertainment and convey aesthetic expression. The first function is important in child learning and socialization, since it guides moral action. A good example of this moral function is found in Navajo narratives about Coyote (Toelken, 1969 and 1975). These trickster tales could be taken as fiction, creation stories, legend or entertainment. Yet for the teller the essence of the narratives lies in the moral and cultural reactions of the audience. The significance is not in the content or structure, but in the texture and style. Social meaning here is far more important than referential meaning. Narrators use a style which provokes audience laughter at Coyote's weakness, excess or stupidity. Laughter becomes the audience's recognition of what they themselves would not do. The story itself promotes this moral assessment. The teller does not need to openly explain or be didactic. A Navajo teller concluded, 'If my children hear the stories, they will grow up to be good people; if they don't hear them, they will turn out to be bad' (Toelken, 1969, p. 221).

This strong moral element is found in one kind of Apache narrative of personal experience (Basso, 1984) which is told in order to modify a recipient's future behaviour and simultaneously reconstitute the tribal tradition. These true narratives are each connected with a feature of the geographical landscape. As members of the culture view a natural scene associated with a past event, they recall the narrative and its moral point becomes a powerful corrective to thinking and behaviour. Through narrative, the surrounding landscape becomes invested with moral values — a visual symbol of cultural norms. Among members, social delinquents need not be criticized or punished — it is sufficient to 'shoot them' with narratives. Apache narratives are moral weapons.

Two other contrasting examples will show how cultural functions of narratives vary, dovetailing with a conversational point: prospectively or retrospectively. Prospectively, Kirshenblatt — Gimblett (1974 and 1975) shows that in East European Jewish culture narratives are very common. Yet they are rarely told for public performances or for their own sake. Rather, the art of telling them is to apply them to a conversational context in which the point of the narrative is relevant. A narrative, typically a parable or personal experience, is told to connect with a subsequent point by analogy. The meaning is in the analogical relationship. Retrospectively, Akinnaso and Ajirotutu (1982) demonstrate how personal narratives in job interviews are told by interviewees as long responses to questions. Again, such narratives are not told for their own sake. They are goal-oriented towards a hoped-for positive outcome of selection for employment and therefore their function must go beyond storytelling. They must be seen, retrospectively, as answers to prior questions and are told to attract positive evaluation.

Performance

A major feature of anthropological studies of narrative is the attention given to the ways of speaking manifest in **performance**. Performance represents a transformation of referential uses of language towards the social and stylistic uses. It is linked with social, emotional, cognitive and moral functions of narratives in different cultural contexts.

In an influential study, Lord (1965) showed that illiterate Yugoslav poet singers did not memorize material verbatim, but rather reconstructed it in performance. Narratives were sung as creative acts using formulae, themes and groups of words to give a different performance of the 'same' tale on various occasions.

Narrative performance is occasioned by the context in which it takes place (Hymes, 1975). It is interpretable, reportable and repeatable (though probably never in exactly the same way). Narrator's assume responsibility to speak in socially appropriate ways to the audience (Bauman, 1975). The narrator assumes accountability to listeners for the way referential, and more especially, stylistic, aspects of narration are enacted. Performance implies a double contract: the narrator promises a performance, hearers promise to be an audience. No narrative is possible without a disposition to listen as much as a disposition to tell. A poor performance is usually followed by an apology either from the teller for an inadequate telling or from the audience for inadequate listening, partial attention or incomplete understanding. It also implies power relationships: the audience submit to narratorial control by the teller, who may scheme to get this power. The Apache narrative type referred to above is a° clear example of this. Some narrators exercise more than narratorial control in performance — a teacher telling children a story or a headteacher recounting a staffroom narrative have wider authority, which may mean that the audience feel obliged to show appreciation whatever the quality of the performance (Maclean, 1988). Performance of a narrative can offer both teller and audience an enhancement of experience and heightened awareness and interest (Bauman, 1977). It may also give a narrative the potential to rearrange social relations, and assist the negotiation of social identity (Bauman, 1986).

There are a number of features of narrative performance (Bauman, 1975; Hymes, 1975). The narrator may use a formula at the Aperture as an entry to a performance mode. Whilst clearly showing and sharing the story, the narrator may momentarily forget the immediate audience. Dialogue may be dramatized by taking both sides. Variety is often a keynote: the narrator may employ a range of stylistic devices, for example, rhyme, parallelism, figurative language, and vary the prosodic patterns of tempo, stress, pitch and intonation. Different paralinguistic features of voice quality and vocalization may be used. Finally — or at the beginning — the narrator may disclaim performance.

Not all of these will be employed in a single narrative and they will vary cross-culturally. Some performance features are likely to cluster round the Peak or Evaluation sections (Longacre, 1976; Labov, 1972; Goffman, 1975). Some performance will be embedded in wider performance frames: a dialogue performed with 'voices' using linguistic and paralinguistic effects must be seen as 'an ongoing performance within a performance' (Maclean, 1988, p. 12). Performance is designed to trigger evaluation by the audience. This presupposes a mutual perception of cultural norms by tellers and hearers (Tsitsipis, 1983). When the audience is involved in performance 'the teller can create their experience, shape reality for them and more effectively communicate the essential message' (Scheub, 1975, p. 363).

Many teachers' narratives have strong performance qualities, most of which are lost on paper: voice quality, gesture, pitch and pace disappear in transcription. Nevertheless, some aspects of performance can be seen in the following examples.

> N10 I've got quite a nice bunch at the moment. They've got a very nice sense of humour. But one . . . I think it was one day last term, I put a row of fossils out, animal fossils, and I put '120 MILLION YEARS OLD' and as one of the kids walked by he started, [SINGS] 'Happy Birthday to you'. That's the sort of sense of humour they've got. It just sort of kills me. It kills me.

The anecdote shows a teacher of 9-year-olds putting out a display of fossils in the classroom with a written notice indicating their age, a standard teaching procedure. A child reacts spontaneously to the notice by singing the Happy Birthday song, showing a sense of humour which the teacher obviously enjoys as part of the teacher–pupil relationship. By giving this in a narrative the teacher has done more than show a verbal appreciation of the children's humour and his own enjoyment of it. The teller does not simply report the child as singing, he sings as the child did. There is no reporting verb; the teacher starts straight in with the song, as the child did. This dramatizes, but there is more: by imitating the child through narrative performance the teacher gives him credit and at the same time gets some himself, as a performer.

Another example of a teacher as teller quoting dramatically occurred in a narrative — the second of a chain of three — which includes a character, the headteacher, being quoted quoting indirectly another character, a particularly disruptive and difficult pupil. The story was performed with all the polish of an experienced raconteur, and had surely been told before.

> N11 There was an occasion where another one — small of stature, little weedy lad — who was a great nuisance, went for the headmaster — well, the headmaster we had in those days — with a knife and this had its funny side because there was another teacher there who managed to grab hold of him and take the knife away. The headmaster said, 'Yes', he said, 'he came for me with knife and called me a bald-headed bastard. "Bastard", I don't mind, but "bald-headed", *I draw the line.*' You know, so it had its funny side, but at the time it was a disaster. We had to do something about it.

No doubt this narrative could have been performed in a very different way to give details of the conflict and to highlight the knife attack, but the purpose of the moment was to emphasize the humour. This, in fact, expresses the teller's perspective on such matters; as he said later, 'Nine times out of ten if you look for humour in a situation it does not become a serious upset.'

An example of performance through dialogue occurred in a narrative about a young child asking his teacher how to spell a word. The seven turns of the dialogue were clearly separated by strong prosodic indications of who was speaking, hardly to be reflected in the layout below. The lack of reporting verbs is, however, apparent, as is the way in which the teacher steps out of performance to explain to the audience that the word was for a spelling book, the kind in which new words are commonly written for the children to learn.

> N12   A funny thing a couple of days ago, a child came up and
> said, 'Can I have pra?'
> This was for his spelling book, you see.
> 'Pra?' I said, 'Pra?'
> 'Yes, pra . . . pra.'
> 'What?'
> 'Pra, yes, pra.'
> 'Well, what sentence do you want it in?'
> 'Well, you know, "Fifty miles pra."'
> Oh dear, oh dear . . .

The Role of the Audience in Performance

Further connections between ways of speaking, cultural aspects of narrative structure and function, and performance can be seen in two examples of Amerindian narratives which illustrate the role of the audience in performance. This might be simply to show understanding, to be entertained and to applaud. But there are cultural contexts where the audience role goes further than this.

Toelken (1969 and 1975) discusses Amerindian concepts of time and space as circular, recurrent, negotiable and adjustable compared with Anglo-American concepts of them as linear, planned, measurable, controllable. These concepts may be part of Navajo narratives in which the plot is not usually considered important. What is said is less important than the saying. Narratives are saturated with repetition, a ritual recycling of structure. Narratives are performed with dramatic intonation, pauses, gestures, facial expressions and body positions. The wording differs with each telling. The narrative is recomposed as the teller works from a knowledge of 'what ought to happen' (Toelken, 1969, p. 221). A narrative told without an audience is reduced to a base summary: a researcher does not necessarily constitute an audience.

The audience's role in trickster tales is to laugh and to recognize that they would not behave as the central characters do. They are led to feel morally superior through their 'correct' interpretation. Toelken (*ibid*, p. 230) concludes that cultural survival is directly related to the audience's ability to impose resources of the mind, ritually directed through narrative, on an otherwise chaotic scene.

Scollon and Scollon (1981 and 1984) present a parallel example of Athabascan narrative performance. Crucial to this telling are the cultural values of mutual respect between narrator and listeners, non-intervention in others' affairs, and the integration of knowledge. Like Navajo narratives, Northern Athabascan ones have four themes, formally marked and grouped into two or four episodes. The marking is signalled by 'and then' . . . 'and then' with pauses which distinguish background and foregrounded information. In a good telling there is negotiated audience involvement. Enactment demands interaction. The narrator's role is to give sufficient background information on a theme for the audience to anticipate the conclusion and provide it in their own words. The 'best' response is to finish what the narrator is saying. In this way 'the listener tells the story' (*ibid*, p. 176). Without the audience response the narrative becomes very long and boring as the narrator increasingly expands the background information, expecting audience completion. Such a narrative is not an independent structural entity which is tailored to performance. Rather, it is born in interaction. It inevitably imposes a view of reality yet maintains respect for the audience's individuality. The listener's integrity is not violated through narrator imposition of meaning — the narrator does not presume to dictate an interpretation. The final structure is a result of joint narrator–audience negotiation through face-to-face interaction. In this culture, oral narrative of personal experience is a highly developed art form. It has functions of entertainment and management of social relations. It is a prime means to acquire knowledge by maximizing the relevance for those who learn, whilst minimizing the threat to their autonomy. The Athabascan narrative is presented in a take-it-or-leave-it manner, without telling the audience too much. Cross-culturally, it can be appreciated that Athabascans may feel that English narratives told with the conventional three episodes are too short or incomplete and a threat to their self-respect and autonomy. English hearers might regard the Athabascan narrative as too long, disorganized, hesitantly told and meaningless. They wait, in vain, for the point they expect. In either case, it can be concluded, the narrative structure, function and meaning and the ways of saying involved in it, are all culturally located.

Folkloristic Approaches to Occupational Narratives

A recent movement in the study of folklore has turned to oral stories of personal experience, showing how these reflect important aspects of society and culture. For example, in traditional patriarchal societies men's stories focus on experiences far away, on military service or labour migration; women's stories, in contrast, are more homebound, focussing on love, marriage or family life (Degh, 1985). Linked to this movement is the study of occupational narratives, where personal accounts of daily life and work have become the focus of ethnographic study. Such occupational narratives have been divided into such categories as: *cautionary tales* of accidents and disasters, which teach hearers how to avoid them by suggesting causes; *stories of newcomers* or tales of new recruits' early days at work and mistakes they make; *reminiscences* of the good old days, recalling a better past at work; *stories of jokes and pranks* played against newcomers or authority figures; *stories of characters and heroes* showing feats of skill and strength, expertise and humour (Santino, 1978a).

Some occupational narratives reflect the teller's position in the organizational structure: stories told by *subordinates* are reported to be about arrogant superiors, where actions are taken to reverse the status, role or expected behaviour; stories by *superordinates* celebrate their own skills and ability, strongly assert the tellers' selves or tell of their rebellion against bureaucracy (Santino, 1978b).

The study of occupational narratives is held to 'provide insight into and an index of the specific challenges and problems that arise in a job' (Santino, 1978a, p. 212). Some of these stories show occupational self-images. Thus pilots' stories portray the tellers as individualistic and assertive, as people who take control (Santino, 1978b), engineers in their own stories are also individualistic, but with a devil-may-care attitude, while trainmen's stories show the tellers as people who cope with problematic situations (Santino, 1978a) and hospital employees tell stories showing competency in emergencies (Berkman, 1978). Women's stories of their experiences in (unspecified) jobs are said to feature low salaries, slow promotion and humiliations (Kalcik, 1975).

Some occupational stories are also reported as having important roles in the culture of organizations, indeed there are claims that stories are so central to organizations that they couldn't function without them (Mitroff and Kilman, 1975). *Organizational sagas* give a collective understanding of the history, rationale and accomplishment of a formally established group, such as a company or a school. Sagas help give individuals in organizations a rationale for their committment to their work (Clark, 1983). Such stories can disseminate and regenerate shared values and motivations and are often sustained and disseminated by informal storytellers and gossips, working through informal networks. Deal (1985) observes how 'In effective companies, managers and employees freely discuss positive stories about philosophy, exploits of heroes and heroines and the success of distinctive practices. These shared stories carry company values' (p. 607). He advocates that school administrators should identify the informal storytellers among their teachers and actively encourage them, in staffrooms or at parties and celebrations, to tell positive stories of children learning or of memorable events and accomplishments. These would inspire their colleagues inside school and convey to outsiders what the school is really about. Storytelling among the teachers would, he says, help to develop a school's cohesive organizational culture.

Bennett uses folklore concepts in her study (1983) of ten '*group sagas*' told by British college teachers in lunchtime gatherings but includes no structural analysis. Bennett distinguishes these group sagas from *anecdotes* or narratives of personal experience by the presence of a central motif, a pictorial or humorous image. Anecdotes in her terms have a verbal encounter as their central concern, rather than this visual tableau. She describes the sagas as being long and polished. They were often jointly produced. Because they are already familar to participants, they are retold in a cryptic, episodic, fragmented manner. There is plenty of repartee during the telling of the saga and laughter as it finishes. The teachers' performative techniques are similar to those of traditional oral taletellers. She concludes that the function of group sagas is a social bonding through enacting a shared past. They are a ritual of entertainment and solidarity, performed in a ritualized manner. But neither the structure, content nor function of the sagas are related by Bennett to the occupation of teaching.

Criticisms of Anthropological Models of Narrative

In relation to the models considered a number of criticisms might be put forward. These models of narrative seem to be more concerned with cultural differences rather than universals. On the other hand, it is important for researchers working with a particular cultural group, such as teachers, to be aware of the kinds of ways in which narratives do vary in order to be in a better position to analyze narratives effectively.

A second criticism is that some anthropological models rely on written texts (for example, Colby 1968a, 1968b; 1973a, 1973b). While this is perfectly valid, the link with oral narratives needs clarifying. Performance models, as seen, focus on oral narratives and, in general, anthropologists are strongly aware of orally-transmitted culture and, naturally enough, they use transcribed versions to facilitate and report their analysis.

A third criticism is that researchers in this discipline focus on the exotic; they study narratives in little known languages using a limited number of informants. There seems to be a lack of studies of more dominant social-economic groups telling narratives. However, Bauman (1986), Tannen (1980), Heath (1983) and others have studied English speakers' narratives in America with significant numbers of speakers.

Further, these models might be held to take insufficient account of cognitive dimensions of narrative and to overrate performance features at the expense of consideration of narrative deep structures or factors of memory. However, each discipline has its own strengths, and, after all, in cross-disciplinary research it is possible to include such areas, if this is desired.

Implications for an Analysis of Teachers' Narratives

Different cultural groups often have different 'ways of speaking' including ways of narrating. Teachers, as an occupational group with their own cultural patterns of communication, will have their own particular narrative ways. Some distinct uses in *what* is recounted, *how* it is narrated and what teachers *believe* about narration can be expected. In this regard, what is not said, but is understood, is as important as what is recorded. All narratives seem to be structured, but there can be some cultural variation in the realization of those structural possibilities. In the range of narrative functions it can be anticipated that teachers' narratives will have functions of self and cultural identity, entertainment, news, moral evaluation and so on. The concept of performance may not seem appropriate to staffroom narration, yet many staffroom narratives, and those told by teachers at conferences, meetings, and even occasionally in interviews, are performed. More obviously, many teachers do act, entertain and perform stories to younger children as part of their work. Therefore performed narratives, which in a sense are the full, most lively form, may well be found among primary teachers. The performance features listed earlier will facilitate identification of performance and provide a strong link with the Evaluation section of teachers' narratives.

In considering teachers' 'ways of saying', the balance between referential and social meaning needs to be taken into account. If the content of teachers' narratives seems trite, it may be that the social or moral meaning (among teachers) is more important, as was seen in Amerindian narratives. It is likely that part of the social meaning will reside in the tellers' reactions both *within* the narrative and *to* the narrative, in the hearers' reactions both to the *narrative* and to the *narration* and its performance; and in the *interaction* between those present during narration. The style and mode of performance of teachers telling a narrative in the staffroom are likely to be cultural signals of social and professional identity; group membership as a teacher or as a particular type of teacher; and solidarity with fellow practitioners, the audience.

Teachers' narratives can be viewed as reflections of teachers' culture, but narrative is also a medium of culture and the process and performance of narration creates cultural contexts. Listening to, appreciating and performing narratives in the staffroom is one way of being, becoming and feeling like a teacher. Alluding to and recalling previously recounted narratives, sometimes as group sagas, reinforces practical understanding and professional identity through a viewing of the symbolic landscape of past teaching successes, failures, difficulties encountered and problems solved. Practical knowledge, social and moral values are transmitted referentially and stylistically through narrative as much among professional groups, such as teachers, as among cultural groups, tribes and peoples the world over.

Chapter 7

Primary Teachers' Narratives: One Thousand Stories from the Classroom

Most studies of teachers' narratives, as shown in chapter 1, are qualitative in nature. They focus on one or two teachers using biographical or interview approaches, often complemented with classroom observation. Some attempt rich descriptions and analyses of teachers' life stories, showing links between personal and professional self-development in the course of teachers' careers. Others see the power of story-making in teachers' classroom activity and investigate how teachers use key narrative images in their thinking or develop their own narratives to give the curriculum coherence. In most cases the time required for a succession of interviews, writing and summarizing biographies and conducting observations in the classroom necessarily means that small samples are involved. In the long term, of course, a series of such narrative studies, each involving a couple of teachers, can be thought of collectively as moving in a quantitative direction by the accumulation of small-scale studies.

There are, perhaps, several ways to balance the qualitative studies with quantitative data in order to examine the general applicability of findings and insights. One way is to increase the number of interviewers by training teams of researchers to use an interview schedule and research approach and thus draw on a much wider range of teachers' narratives.

Another way is to study the written journals of pre-service teachers or experienced teachers on educational courses, restricting the accounts to written narrative. Since there are often large numbers of teachers on such courses a substantial quantity of data could be gathered.

A further way is to interview teachers using an interview approach which, whilst eliciting narratives of classroom experience, would be less time-consuming than the in-depth interviewing usually used in narrative research. This would allow a larger number of teachers to be involved. Although some detail and depth would be sacrificed, a briefer interview could, it is suggested, still allow teachers to tell narratives giving their cultural perceptions of what it means to be a teacher. None of these ways are exclusive. They could be combined, not only with each other but, more interestingly, with other approaches to research in education.

The third approach is the one which will be elaborated on here. The study to be reported was carried out by a single interviewer and used narrative analysis of teachers' anecdotes to build up a picture of the teachers' world, as portrayed through the teachers' own voices (Cortazzi, 1989 and 1991). The general approach was the 'teacher's anecdotes' method referred to in chapter 1.

A Study of British Primary Teachers' Narratives

This study was based on interviews with 123 British primary teachers, working in eleven different schools. In the majority of the schools the entire staff were interviewed. One or two teachers were absent during the time that the researcher was in their school. One person refused to be interviewed and one refused to be tape-recorded. Ninety-five of the 123 teachers were female. This was not surprising, given the fact that many taught 5–8-year-olds in the schools, and it is much less usual for male teachers to work with that age group. The age range of the teachers involved was evenly spread across the career-span, with a slight over-representation of teachers in their late forties. Most of the teachers were very experienced: only eighteen had taught for less than three years, ninety had over five years experience, including twenty-three who had been teaching for more than twenty-one years.

Each teacher was interviewed individually for about thirty minutes. The interviews were recorded, carefully listened to later and any narratives were transcribed. This procedure yielded the main data base of 856 narratives. All the teachers told at least one narrative, most told between four and ten narratives, one teacher recounted seventeen.

To supplement these interview data, an additional 105 narratives recorded among teachers' groups were considered. These were told in teachers' meetings (staff meetings, conferences, seminars and workshops) by teachers talking to known colleagues, in groups of between five and twenty-five teachers. Thus there is a total of 961 narratives — nearly 1000. This is a substantial collection of teachers' anecdotes, giving a data base considerably larger than previous research (see chapter 1).

The Interviews

The interviews elicited narratives by using a semi-structured approach. They took place in the staffroom, medical room or in teachers' classrooms if children were absent. That the staffs of the eleven schools were willing to undergo the disruption entailed by the interview process indicates strong support. The teachers were informed that the purpose of the research was to ask about teachers' day-to-day experiences in order to build up a picture of what teaching is really like. Teachers were interested and helpful. Frequent comments were, 'At last someone is asking us' or 'If you could give a proper picture, perhaps people would appreciate what teachers do.'

In the interviews, teachers were asked a few questions and encouraged to give examples from their day-to-day teaching. The basic questions were:

— What happened yesterday/last week? Was it a typical day? Did anything unusual happen?
— What are the children like in your class this year? Do any children stand out?
— Have any of the children in your class had a breakthrough recently?
— Have you ever had any trouble with parents?
— Have you ever had any disasters in teaching?
— What is the funniest thing that has ever happened to you in teaching?

Some of these questions are similar, of course, to Labov's 'Danger of Death' or 'Most Embarrassing Moment' questions (1972) which generally elicit stories from respondents.

In their answers, teachers were encouraged to give examples from their experience, but no mention was made of 'stories', 'anecdotes' or 'narratives'. At the end of the interview teachers were asked if they had, in fact, given a good picture of teaching. Most of them unhesitatingly affirmed that they had, a few added extra comments; none said that they had not or that it was not possible to give a picture of teaching in thirty minutes or so. Somehow, asking about these topics and giving teachers plenty of opportunity to talk about their own experience allowed them to present what they said was a good picture of teaching.

Many narratives were performed, especially through quoted dialogue. Teachers animated their stories with gestures and prosody, using great variation in pitch ranges and intonation patterns, (noticeably more than in their normal speech) and adopting different tones of voice and accents to imitate children. This gave many stories an emotional tone of fondness for children, even of identification with children. There were frequent performed switches between child and adult roles. Two further features were interesting: an incessant 'you know' which framed citations in reported teacher–pupil dialogue which, among other things, seemed to convey a strong feeling of typicality of the quoted words; and a frequent quotation of teachers' thinking, 'I thought, "....."'. These features give a general feeling that in their narratives the tellers were in effect saying, 'This is how it is', 'This is how I talk to the children and they talk to me' and 'This is how I teach'.

Narrative Analysis

The collected narratives were categorized according to topic and then analyzed using the evaluation model discussed in chapter 2 (Labov and Waletsky, 1967; Labov, 1972). This model was chosen because the Evaluation section draws attention to the tellers' perspectives on the meaning of the narrative for the speaker. If a large number of Evaluations are collected on the same topic this allows an exploration of teachers' cultural perspectives. This goes considerably beyond Labov's use of the model. The method of analysis was to read through the narratives analyzing them according to the structure: Abstract, Orientation, Complication, Resolution, Coda, Evaluation. Any striking or common features about the contents, language or structure were noted. Then all Abstracts, Orientations and Evaluations of narratives on the same topic were grouped in order to look for common perspectives. The Abstract, it will be recalled, signals an upcoming narrative and often summarizes its main point for the speaker; collecting these is a way of distilling speakers' perspectives. The Orientation gives important information about characters and setting; since children feature overwhelmingly as main characters, collecting these is a way of analyzing how teachers refer to different types of children. The Evaluation gives the meaning of the narrative, highlights the speaker's perspective and attitude to what has been told; collecting these is a way of analyzing speakers' perspectives. With a few narratives the perspectives revealed may possibly be individual or situational ones. However, if the same perspectives are evident in the narratives of a number of teachers, then this would be evidence that the perspectives may be cultural, pertaining to groups of teachers. Analyzing many narratives told by a large sample of teachers, working in different schools, in this way gives some confidence that any common perspectives found are cultural, part of the teachers' occupational culture. An example will illustrate this procedure.

An Example of the Analysis

N13

A   Sometimes I'll just come in and think, 'Oh no, I'm fed up with them, doing maths and English all the time and they are as well' and I just think of something on the spur of the moment.

O   Just before half term, a couple of weeks before half term, they were doing maths, English, maths, English, week in, week out, the same old stuff

C   so I came in after break and I thought, 'This isn't good enough. We'll have to do something different' and I thought, 'Let's try Star Turn.' It just sort of struck me, you know, as I walked through the door. So they got on with their normal work for about ten minutes and all of a sudden I started dragging, getting all these different things together and I dragged that fire extinguisher across the floor and dumped some things, a bowl of wallpaper and a bottle of ink and all this sort of thing, and the kids must have thought I'd gone mad or something. So I put out seven chairs in a circle and they suddenly realized what I was going to do and they were all excited about this and I put one object on each chair and explained what we were going to do, you know. They had thirty seconds each and at the end of thirty seconds I blow the whistle

E   and it was absolutely amazing what I got from them, you know, they were all so eager to try this, even the kind of kids who are normally very quiet. It was absolutely amazing the story lines and the imagination I got from them, you know, and they really enjoyed it

Coda   and we did it a couple of times and we're going to do it this week

E   and I think that must be one of the best lessons that I've ever had, just sort of off the spur of the moment and they really enjoyed it and got some good things out of it. It's the first thing I'd actually done where I could get them to express themselves and talk and explain things, you know, and I was absolutely amazed.

A teacher's 'best lesson', such as this, is likely to have salient importance in defining that practitioner's personal parameters of what 'works well'. A narrative analysis can reveal the teacher's perspectives by looking particularly at the Abstract — which shows what the anecdote will be about — and the Evaluation — which reveals the teller's perspective on what has been told. These will then be compared with other Abstracts and Evaluations of narratives told by other teachers, or this one, on the same or similar topics. The structure of the narrative could be analyzed in much finer detail, particularly in the Complication, but the broad divisions shown will give the idea.

The Abstract, or opening summary, here contrasts the teacher's and pupils' feelings of boredom from routine work with a lesson planned 'on the spur of the moment': the point of interest is the spontaneity and success of the lesson, both of which seem closely linked.

The Evaluation, picked out by emphasis, repetition, use of adverbs and explanation, highlights three elements. First, that this was a best lesson, done spontaneously. Unlike the routine lessons which the teacher was 'fed up with', this lesson aroused interest and excitement. There seem to be two perspectives, which if held by many teachers would be important cultural perspectives, that the best lessons are not planned and that the teacher's and children's interest and sense of excitement are important factors in successful teaching.

Second, that the teller was 'amazed' at what he 'got from them'. This is emphasized by the triple repetition and by the use of the qualifier 'absolutely' each time. What he 'got from them' and what they 'got out of it' are not specified beyond 'imagination' and 'story lines' and the fact that the lesson is about 'creative' expression. Again, if there were more examples, 'getting imagination out of children' could be an important perspective revealing something of teachers' concepts of learning, possibly contrasted with learning skills, developing processes, concepts, understanding or attitudes.

Third, the pupils' enjoyment, seen in the repeated 'they really enjoyed it'. As a criterion for a successful lesson this is another important perspective which again may contrast with unmentioned areas of learning, such as knowledge, concepts, and so on.

Some of the general results of this study are now given, summarized according to the topic of the narratives.

Stories of Outstanding Individuals

There were 105 narratives about children who stand out. The Orientations of these contained many typifications of children which on analysis could be reduced to three types. These seemed to be cultural models for viewing children in classrooms. Outstanding children were seen as academic, problems or characters. The *academic* model was essentially 'two extremes with the majority in the middle', as one teacher said. This is a linear model, with 'bright', 'able', 'high fliers' 'at the top', as many teachers said; the 'middle third' of 'the average ones' who were 'in between'; and the 'not so bright', 'backward', 'slower learning ones', 'at the tail'. A concern, expressed by twenty teachers, was that 'the middle band tend to fade'. 'They don't stand out enough'. This group is 'overlooked', 'difficult to know', 'pushed into the background' and 'forgotten' in 'that middle sort of grey area'. In the *problem* model, teachers saw some children who *caused* them problems as 'naughty', 'troublesome children' who were 'a nuisance', and other children who *had* problems, invariably because of their home situation. In the *character* model, children stood out because they were 'the characters', 'with outgoing personalities', 'with a sense of humour', who 'each have something nice about them'.

Polarities in Primary Teaching

In attempting to distil the essence of the teachers' cultural perceptions of their work as shown in the narratives, ten binary oppositions or *polarities* can be suggested, not unlike the Berlak's 'dilemmas of schooling' (1981) or Pollard's concept of teachers' role factors (1985), although the source of these polarities is quite different. All ten polarities are shown in table 22, but each will be introduced after presenting a brief idea of the narrative data which led to it.

The assumption is that both poles of each opposition are necessary to teaching and that the relationship between each pole is one of dynamic tension, rather than of choice. The mention of some of these was natural, following a particular interview question. However, the analysis of the teachers' cultural perceptions which follows is derived from the teachers' narratives, not from any other kind of answer to the questions.

The first of these polarities is the *individual–class* polar opposition. This summarizes a problem of class teachers: they work with class groups within a tradition of education which emphasizes individuals. At different times teachers need to focus either on individuals or on the whole class. The narratives clearly indicate, however, that only *some* individuals stand out in teachers' perceptions: for academic ability, problems or character. These few individuals apparently dominate the teacher's consciousness of the class. They may dictate much of the pace and style of classroom work.

Stories of Awkward Parents

In this sample there were 126 stories about parents who were 'awkward'. Typically, problems which were reported with these parents were the result of misunderstandings or having different perspectives, for example, whereas the parents focus on one child, the teacher has to take thirty children into account. Some parents could become 'irate', 'rude', 'abusive' or 'aggressive'. These parents were a minority, but it was a minority which seemed to have an important effect on teachers' thinking. The parents often came to school in 'Storm' metaphors. In the teachers' narratives they 'came storming in', 'came storming down', 'came storming up' or 'came storming back'. They were 'ramping and raving away' or 'shouting the odds'. Parents 'created hell', 'threatened to come and bash my brains in' and were 'coming up to school to punch that teacher on the nose'. Actual violence was usually avoided by tactful headteachers who placated the parents with explanations. In the vast majority of cases it was the parents who were portrayed as being clearly in the wrong. The Resolutions in these narratives come about through teachers' explanations — not those of parents. This showed a marked asymmetry of perception: things got 'sorted out' both in and on the teachers' terms. Any apologies given later came from parents.

This second polarity, the *parent–teacher* polarity, captures a potential conflict area. While in their narratives, teachers see the importance of knowing a child's home background and eliciting support from parents, yet when pupils have behavioural, social or other problems teachers tend to view the source of this as being in the home, at the parent pole. With the few awkward parents, teachers often need to explain their own situation to resolve difficulties. They switch from the need to know the home of the individual child to the need to explain their concerns for the whole class to the parent.

Stories of Being Flexible

Teachers affirmed the need to plan but there were 116 narratives about lessons which indicated the need to 'play it by ear' because something 'cropped up'. Teachers thus often followed the children's 'interest', 'excitement' or 'enjoyment'. This was frequently associated with the perceived need for the children 'to talk about it'. The clear picture was of the need to be flexible in adapting to children's shifting attention or to follow their interest or experience. This can be seen in the following example.

N14   Sometimes I do play it by ear because so many interesting things do crop incidentally, because I've got an interesting class. Well, one boy, for example, is very interested in car racing. This comes from the fact that his father manages some racing cars and we were discussing the design of the car and I realized that Mark knows considerably more about it than I did, so I stayed at the back of the room ... and said, 'Mark, it's all yours', you know, 'We'll ask you questions that you'll give us the answers to', you know, 'Why are tyres thick?' 'Why do we have this?' 'Why are they made like that?' It went very well, very well. Topic work can come up incidentally, a child can bring a book along, an interesting book about birds or something, and some children then become inspired and would like to do some work on birds. Fine! That's the time to let them take off, when the interest and enthusiasm are there.

Flexibility–planning is a third polarity, where teachers' statements about the need to plan teaching were generally offset by other statements about the need to be flexible. All the narratives in this category were about being flexible in order to follow children's interests when something 'cropped up'.

Breakthrough Stories

How teachers see one aspect of children's learning, 'a breakthrough' is shown in ninety-six narratives collected on this topic. Teachers, especially primary teachers, spend most of their working day with the same group of children, who, we hope, are learning. Experienced teachers therefore have ample opportunity to be with children when the actual moments of learning occur. How do British primary teachers perceive children's learning? How do they describe those moments? How do they explain them? Here are some examples of breakthrough stories.

N15   One boy that I've had a lot of trouble with, his reading is not good, but his number was appalling. He couldn't count, he couldn't recognize any numbers and then all of a sudden in the space of about two weeks it seemed to click and I could see him beginning to go. He's now beginning to understand it. It suddenly came on ...

N16   And then another little boy who just did not understand addition at all. I tried it all ways. You name it, I tried it and then all of a sudden he just came in one day and [clicks fingers] it seemed to click and I could really see the breakthrough.

Such accounts could easily be dismissed as anecdotal — interesting but unimportant slices of classroom life, small experiences of the tellers which do not constitute evidence in research terms. However, when a large number of these accounts of breakthroughs in learning are collected and analyzed it becomes clear that there are common patterns in both the content and in the ways of telling. These patterns are evidence of common experience and perception and, perhaps, of thinking.

Within these teachers' stories of children's learning, the actual moment of learning is characteristically described in images: a large number of teachers repeatedly use a limited range of metaphors in the Evaluations, shown in table 20 from Cortazzi (1991, pp. 50–2). (Numbers in brackets refer to the number of teachers using an expression where there was more than one.)

These are the dominant metaphors which this group of primary teachers use to describe learning in their narrative accounts of classroom experience. There are no references to learning theories as taught in education or psychology courses. Rather, it seems that on the basis of their knowledge of children and their experience of working with them, teachers construct their own folk-theories or cultural models, based on generalized event-schemata. These emerge when teachers recount particular memories of children learning, and they emerge built round metaphors. Not, it seems, using a wide range of metaphors — a restricted number are used with great frequency.

In few of the narratives is there an explanation for the learning beyond 'giving extra attention'. More usually, the breakthrough is unexplained. It remains magical and mysterious. It is, in the teachers' words, 'accidental', 'by coincidence', 'just one of those things'. It is 'unbelievable', 'unpredictable', 'there's no reason . . . it just happens'.

The model of learning which can be distilled from analyzing ninety-six stories about breakthroughs in children's learning is shown in table 21. There is first a struggle with learning: the teacher tries various methods but the learner is so far unsuccessful. In the narratives the teller often shares thoughts or feelings about this which reportedly occurred to him/her at the time. Then something 'clicks' or 'light dawns'. This happens suddenly, or at least, it is noticed suddenly. Then there is a moment of joy, where again the teller is very likely to share thoughts and emotions about the event. The teacher expresses surprise, amazement

Table 20: *Teacher's Metaphors for Learning, from Narratives*

LEARNING AS A CLICK (28)
— it clicks (7)
— it all clicked (2)
— it began to click (2)
— it seemed to click (3)
— everything seemed to sort of click
— it just clicked together
— it just simply clicked (2)
— it has all just clicked (2)
— it's clicked in his mind
— there was a sort of click in their minds
— he has clicked
— it must have just clicked
— it all clicked straight away
— it's beginning to click
— the words clicking and the number clicking
— hoping that one of the ways will click

LEARNING AS LIGHT (18)
— the light dawns (5)
— it dawned on him
— daylight has dawned at last
— he saw the light (2)
— he's seen the light
— they see the light
— the light in his eyes
— their eyes light up
— the light on their face
— her face lit up
— he really saw it
— a spark
— this sort of flash going straight through

LEARNING AS MOVEMENT (50)
— it's come
— he/she came on (6)
— he's come round
— she's just come out

— she came from nothing
— they've come through
— they're beginning to go
— I could see him beginning to go
— they're not going to move that much
— he is just beginning to move
— they've moved at the same time
— they all seemed to be moving
— she's gone
— he has suddenly gone on
— she just goes straight through
— we've got through
— you get through (2)
— he got off on his reading
— a couple really have pushed through
— one child has made a step forward
— the child reaches forward and meets you
— he/she made great leaps and bounds (3)
— her achievements went up in leaps and bounds
— this sudden leap
— we really have got lift off point with her
— they take off again
— this girl has suddenly taken off
— the least able child has reached a milestone
— he came to a peak
— he was off, he was off
— she was running away with her reading
— making great strides with his reading
— we've made it
— we've got somewhere
— he whipped through
— they zoomed away
— they go great guns
— you can see a spurt forward
— they do learn in these spurts
— she was making headway
— he made quite a bit of headway
— they had a surge

Table 21: *The Teachers' Experience of Breakthroughs in Children's Learning*

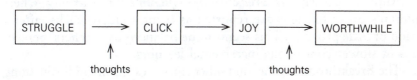

127

and wonder and thinks that this is what makes teaching worthwhile and rewarding — it is worth the struggle. The double likelihood of teachers expressing their thoughts at defined points in these narratives well illustrates Bruner's (1986) suggestion that narratives have two landscapes: a world of action and a world of consciousness, which portrays the minds of protagonists or the narrator's subjectivity. How teachers think, as they report in stories when they are presumably concentrating on the narrative, can thus be indirectly investigated through narrative analysis.

This kind of model of learning is illustrated by two further stories which are built around metaphors.

N17　One particular girl, she suddenly realized she was making headway and the whole of her outlook on school work changed dramatically because of that, and her achievements went up in leaps and bounds. It may have had something to do with teacher expectations as well. She has suddenly taken off with her reading and other things. I was sat there, I must have looked daft because I had a silly grin all over my face and I was so pleased with this and that was my reward for the day, that she had achieved and that she had somehow managed to get herself going. I think any little thing that a child doesn't understand and is genuinely worried about and comes to you and says to you, 'I don't understand this. I can't make head or tail of it'. And if they go away and they can understand it, you can see the light dawn on their face and that to me is worth — well, you can't put a worth on it in financial terms.

N18　You get lots of small instances. I think you share in the child's delight in that. I can think of lots of little instances where you've been plugging away, particularly with reading, sometimes with writing, where they've struggled, you've helped and you've felt for months and months that you've made very little progress and suddenly it dawns on you that the child is improving. Suddenly the reading is coming on and the smile that dawns on that child's face when they appreciate that they can read. It's a most exciting moment.

Another polarity is *breakthrough–incremental learning* where children's breakthroughs are reported as being sudden 'clicks' after a period of little progress. This seems to be balanced by teachers' perceptions of slower continuous incremental learning.

The Breakthrough stories and other stories, especially in Evaluations, showed that teachers found their job rewarding and worthwhile because of their relationships with children, typically seen in 'small' moments when a child suddenly learned something, or said something funny, or showed interest and enjoyment. This was in spite of a strong perception of increasing social pressures and problems, articulated most clearly by headteachers. In narratives, teachers presented themselves as being devoted to their work and highly motivated to teach children, at a time of low salaries and low morale.

Disaster Stories

There were 124 Disaster stories. Many of these described accidents, things going wrong with organization or problems with discipline and control. Many showed teachers learning from things going wrong: the disasters were admissible, perhaps, precisely because the teacher had learnt and would know how to avoid possible disasters in future. Many showed teachers coping under difficult circumstances, struggling to maintain competence or face. Disaster stories essentially show how teachers respond to disasters, as in the following example:

N19 I've seen loads of disasters with plays and things. We've always managed to get it right for whenever we've put it on but we've had some terrible things go wrong on the way. I think the most horrifying thing is when kids don't turn up on the night. This has happened. I know, having worked with these kids, from experience, from when I first started doing these plays and things. I always now keep a couple of kids near me, some of the better ones, if you like, who are just singing in the choir or just doing some little things that can easily . . . I just turn round and say, 'OK you do this.' And I've told them as we've gone along what things to watch. We did an Arts Development thing over at the Sports Centre and I was asked to do the mime. So we piled in the kids and worked on it and made masks and we had to go to a full rehearsal and on that day two of the key parts didn't turn up. So we got there and there was one part we couldn't do without and there were loads of schools there and the orchestra was full and this was kind of the high spot and these kids were doing the action to this song and one of the girls, who is in my class and who is very good, she was just sitting there. She was in the choir . . . and er I just suddenly

... it was all very quiet and everything, I suddenly said, 'Oh, would you come down.' She was looking around. She came down and I said, 'Go on then. You've watched it. Off you go. Don't worry about it.' And she went through it and I don't think anyone knew she'd never done it before. But I must admit I was really on the line. But every time we'd practised it I'd always said to her, 'you make sure that you watch and be prepared to fill in.'

The teller indicates that organization can go wrong in teaching situations. Sometimes this is outside the teachers' control, yet the narrative makes the basic point that teachers can make provision for mishaps: teachers can overcome 'the most horrifying thing' of children not turning up. The disaster is recounted to the teacher's credit because it shows his preparation of the understudy, after, it is implied, previous disasters. The school rehearsal is, in fact, a performance since 'loads of schools were there' watching. The teacher's reaction to the emergency is calm. On tape, he says very quietly, in a calm voice, 'Oh, would you come down?' Since this stands out dramatically, this is part of the Evaluation. The girl, aged 8, rises to the emergency, very successfully. The teacher, however, does not evaluate her performance on the stage, no details of which are given. Rather he evaluates his reaction by emphasizing how he had prepared beforehand, though he was still 'on the line'. The story presents him as calm and able to handle any such emergency. Professionally, he remains in control.

Disaster–stability is a further polarity. Many disasters were reported as unanticipated interruptions to stability. Disasters in narratives were of various types, ranging from mild accidents to severely disturbing incidents. The teacher's response to these must be to restore stability. The majority of disasters in narratives occurred with individual children, potentially disrupting the stability of the whole class. When disasters with the class were recalled these were invariably lessons that had gone awry.

Humorous Stories

Out of 168 humorous narratives, the vast majority were centred on children: sixty-two being about the amusing remarks which children unintentionally make, fifty-two being about humorous actions, thirty-five about disasters which had a funny side, eleven concerning children's written howlers, the remainder being teachers' remarks or about funny situations. Thirty-nine teachers spontaneously remarked on the frequency of humorous events in their classroom, for example, 'Humorous things happen all the time', 'It's a laugh a minute, really.' As with the stories of breakthroughs in children's learning, it became clear that for these British primary teachers these laughs are important. They are transient in their nature, yet enduring in memory: 'That I'll never forget', 'These are the sorts of things that stick out in your mind', 'It is one of the most memorable moments of my teaching career.' They were an important part of what made teaching worthwhile.

Laughter–seriousness is another polarity, an opposition between the assumed serious tone of most teaching activity and the smiles and laughter which frequently arise, mostly from children's incongruous sayings and doings. Classroom humour is always unexpected, usually associated with an individual child, and a key element in teachers' job satisfaction.

Further Polarities

Some other polarities can be adduced from the range of narratives. In the polarity of *unpredictability–routine*, the expected routine of planned, serious, normal classroom work is contrasted with the unpredictable, the unexpected and variety. Not surprisingly, there are few narratives about the somewhat unnewsworthy routine element in teaching. However, there are literally hundreds of unpredictable elements in the entire range of the teachers' narratives. Teachers commented that such variety made teaching interesting and enjoyable. It was, in fact, said by many to be typical. Therefore it can be argued that this polarity is characteristic of teachers' cultural perceptions and not an artefact of narrative production.

In the polarity of *enjoyment–grind*, teaching was reported as being 'hard work', a 'grind', 'slog' or 'struggle'. Yet narratives were also permeated with enjoyment, when frequently teachers were 'amazed', 'thrilled' or 'had great fun'. This was often shared with children and was nearly always derived from working with children.

Another polarity is *social–cognitive*. This expresses two key aspects of education which might both be expected to feature in teachers' narratives. In fact, there are few references to the cognitive pole. Even in narratives specifically about children's learning few details are given about exactly what was learnt, or how. In contrast, the social pole is continually mentioned: Teachers repeatedly stress children's 'interest', 'involvement', 'enjoyment', 'excitement'. Classroom relationships and children's social situations at home are continually referred to.

A final polarity is *general–technical*, which refers to the teachers' use of language registers in narratives. Technical or academic terms are completely avoided, even in narrative topics such as children's learning, where some professional or technical terms might be expected. Perhaps teachers were perfectly capable of using technical language, as they must do on occasion in the classroom, but narrative does not demand it. Such an interpretation would fit in with Bruner's (1986) distinction between *logico-scientific thinking* and *narrative*, where the first deals with issues of truth observation, analysis and proof, while the second deals with issues of human experience, beliefs, doubts, emotions and intentions.

The teachers' use of metaphor is an obvious case of using general terms in contexts which would otherwise demand technical language. The metaphors are so frequent in use, yet so limited in range, that they appear to constitute a folk terminology for learning. Metaphors seem to enable verbalization about the unknown or inexplicable, yet they may also inhibit deeper reflection and professional development. To say 'it clicked', or 'her face lit up' or 'she really came on in leaps and bounds' is certainly meaningful as metaphorical description, but without further analysis it does seem limited as a professional way of focussing on one of the central issues of education — children's learning.

This is the point at which the anecdotal method of this research should be combined with, or extended by, other approaches such as the curriculum inquiry method (see chapter 1), so that having identified a key area like this use of metaphors the researcher goes back to the teachers to explore with them further implications of the narratives.

Table 22 summarizes the polarities which seem to be at work in the teachers' narrative accounts of their work.

Semiotic Squares

Larger patterns of narrative meanings in the teachers' stories can be expressed as semiotic squares, in which more complex structures or relations of meaning can be shown.

In a *semiotic square*, as shown in chapter 4, horizontal dimensions are contraries, vertical ones are complementary and diagonal ones are contradictory. The examples given below are in effect summaries of major aspects of the cultural perspectives found in the teachers' narratives.

The square in table 23 expresses key aspects of teachers' cultural

Table 22:   Teachers' Polarities

individual . . . . class
parent . . . . teacher
flexibility . . . . planning
breakthrough . . . . incremental learning
disaster . . . . stability
humour . . . . seriousness
unpredictability . . . . . . routine
enjoyment . . . . grind
social . . . . cognitive
general . . . . technical

Table 23:   Teachers' Perceptions of Children

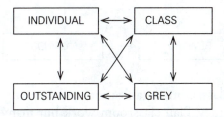

perceptions of children. Teachers express the need to see children as Individuals, meeting individual needs. Large numbers of Individuals make a Class, the demands of which override those of Individuals, as teachers tell parents. Since there is clearly a tension between the Individual and the Class that can be expressed as contraries. Outstanding children combine aspects of both Individual and Class. They are particularly salient individuals who readily come to teachers' minds, often years later. They are the ultimate Individuals, seen in terms of a limited number of cultural models held by teachers: children who stand out for academic ability, problems they bring or for their character. These Individuals dominate the teacher's consciousness of the Class. In their absence the Class is noticeably different. They are the extremes, who to a large extent seem to determine the pace, style, management and mood of the class and the teacher's relationship to it. The Grey children are 'in the middle'. They are neither Individuals nor the Class, though they are of it. They do not stand out. If they are absent the effect is negligible. Quiet workers, they are easily overlooked or forgotten. Many teachers are aware of overlooking the Grey children, but do not seem to have strategies available for giving them attention.

A second square, shown in table 24 summarizes aspects of teachers'

Table 24: *Teachers' Perceptions of Planning and Learning*

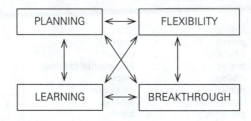

Table 25: *Teachers' Perceptions of Aspects of their Work*

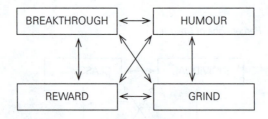

perceptions of classroom organization and learning. Teachers invariably affirm that they Plan classroom work but many narratives are all about Flexibility — responding immediately to children's interests and enjoyment when things 'crop up'. Learning combines both, since much learning is Planned, yet the more memorable instances of Learning and the most successful lessons in teachers' stories come from the Flexible response of 'playing it by ear'. A Breakthrough involves neither Planning nor Flexibility since narratives reveal the fortuitous, sudden, unpredictable nature of the Breakthrough and yet Breakthroughs are not exploited for children's interest in the way in which things which 'crop up' are. Breakthroughs invariably occur with Individuals in teachers' stories. In contrast, Learning can be assumed to take place with all children most of the time. A Breakthrough is a kind of Learning but it is outside the teacher's control. Flexibility originates with children but it is ultimately controlled by the teacher. Teachers seem to reflect very little on the reasons for successful Flexible lessons or learning in Breakthroughs.

The third square, shown in table 25 expresses some of the social and cognitive ups and downs of teachers' perceptions of their work with children. Breakthroughs and Humour have the common feature of being unpredictable and outside the teacher's control, but they are contraries to the extent that Breakthroughs are cognitive affairs, while classroom Humour is a social event. Both Breakthroughs and Humour are key elements in the Rewards for teachers — many teachers specifically say as much in their stories. The Grind aspect of teaching is the hard slog, when there are no apparent Breakthroughs and Humour has not arisen. A Breakthrough is preceded by a Grind, yet the Breakthrough itself is not a Grind, rather it is sudden excitement which contradicts the Grind. Humour is vital to offset the Grind. Where the Breakthrough and Grind are primarily cognitive, the Humour and Reward are primarily social.

The Teacher's Self

The notion of the teacher's self has been clearly linked with narrative in education (see chapter 1), where many commentators have observed how narrative links the personal and professional self. It will be recalled also that Goffman (1975) showed how narrators may present themselves as author, principal or source for impression management (see chapter 2). These distinctions parallel those of Genette (1980) and others between speaking subject, narrating subject, subject of narration and narrated subject in literary models, where narrators focalize through different selves for narrative effect (see chapter 4). Distinct selves are central to such models of narrative.

This notion of distinct selves has also been put forward as central to teachers' methods for coping and managing interests-at-hand (Pollard, 1985). The central importance of self-image as distinct from professional image has also been stressed (Nias, 1989), while both of these notions have been examined in relation to teachers' life history to see how they find expression in a curriculum area (Woods, 1990). Teaching demands much self-investment (of talent, personality, skills and ideas) and much self-expression. Pupils and classroom events can confirm or threaten a teacher's image of professional competence (Nias, 1989, p. 55) or that teacher's personal self-image (Pollard, 1985, p. 237). It is therefore natural to draw a distinction between a teacher's self as part of the professional role and the teacher's self as a person. Of the two, the second may have more importance for many teachers, since as many as 80 per cent of teachers in their first decade of teaching apparently do not feel like professionals but do feel, and need to feel, a sense of self (Nias, 1989, p. 38).

These distinct selves of teachers emerged also in the narratives analyzed here. An attempt to distil further the cultural perceptions of self shown in the teachers' narratives yields a 'square of squares' as shown in table 26.

Table 26:   A Control-Orientation Model of Teaching

	Control	**Orientation**
External	SIGNIFICANT EVENTS	SIGNIFICANT OTHERS
Self	PROFESSIONAL ROLE	TEACHER AS PERSON

The left-hand squares represent significant classroom events and actions which are within the teacher's locus of control. The teacher's role is controllable. It expresses the teacher's professional self. The right-hand squares represent the orientation of the teacher to significant others, who are sometimes unpredictable and outside the teacher's control, and the orientation of the teacher to his/her own self, as a person. The latter, at social and emotional levels, may be less easily controlled than the professional self. The notion of control implies controlling learning as well as controlling order.

This model represents not only an interpretation of the trajectory of a substantial number of individual narratives but of classes of narratives. The patterns of different classes of narrative can be traced through the square.

In Breakthrough stories, Orientations depict the teacher as trying to help a child, attempting to control the significant event of learning. In a sense, the child as a significant other is in control. The child is not, apparently, learning. When it occurs, the breakthrough is admittedly outside the teacher's control — if anything it might be controlled by the child. The actual moment of the breakthrough, the 'click', is a significant event described in the Complication. This is recognized by the teacher in role but responded to by the teacher as a person in terms of a 'surprise', 'thrill' or 'enjoyment' in the Evaluation. This emotional response of the personal self makes teaching worthwhile and reinforces social relationships between teacher and pupils. The teacher's self-image of professional competence, which could have been threatened by the non-learning, is restored. The narrative trajectory homes in towards the self at an emotional level in terms of the rewards of teaching.

In stories of being flexible, the role of the teacher is to plan and organize the significant event of classroom activity and learning. In the Complications, something 'crops up', changing the significant event.

This is frequently because something unexpected occurs. The teacher sees the children's interest and 'takes it from there', responding in role by organizing learning around the new, now controlled, significant event. The teacher, in the Evaluation, observes that the children enjoyed it, were interested and excited and herself enjoys it: 'we' enjoyed it, as the teachers say. Again relationships are bonded and threatened disorder from distraction is avoided through the teacher's competence in responding flexibly to children's interests. The personal self has satisfaction with work and the professional self is seen to be competent.

Disaster stories can also be seen in terms of a path through the square. A significant event, a lesson, has been controlled in terms of order and learning. In the Complication this is disrupted by a pupil, as a significant other, having an accident, or by pupils causing a lesson to go awry. The teacher in role copes with the disaster and sometimes with the implied threats of possible comebacks from a parent for negligence. The professional self is relieved, remains competent or in the case of lessons going wrong has learnt from a poor lesson, assuring future competence.

Stories of Awkward Parents frequently have a Complication of a parent, as a significant other, 'storming in' with complaints or threats. This significant event challenges the role of the teacher and therefore the teacher's self-image. Teachers solve this problem in role either by using explanations to clear up misunderstandings or by calling upon another significant person, the headteacher, to ward off threats and deal with complaints. In Evaluations, teachers remain in control and are basically right. The self-image is restored after the comeback. Status and competence are unaffected. The stress and anxieties caused to teachers by awkward parents suggests that the personal self is also threatened, since teachers identity so strongly with their ('my') class, their ('my') children and their work.

Such general patterns subsume many, though not of course all, of the 1000 or so narratives considered. It might be speculatively suggested that the polar oppositions and semiotic squares have correlates in the form of schemata deriving from cultural perspectives and influencing later perceptions of events and the narrating of them.

Further Research

The approaches to narrative analysis discussed here can clearly be developed further. There is no reason why methods and insights from a number of disciplines should not be integrated for any particular research question. This is not usually done, perhaps because of a tendency for academics to work within the scope of a single discipline, often using well-tried research methods. Narrative analysis, as a newer research method, might well be used in conjunction with other methods of educational research. Interview transcripts, for example, could be reexamined in a search for anecdotes and stories — which otherwise would probably be discounted — to investigate their content, structure, function, performance, and genesis in the interview (Mishler, 1986). The important role of the interviewer, or collaborative biographer, in the genesis of stories needs to be considered in the light of the sociolinguistic research on storytelling.

The various current approaches to using narrative in education, such as the development of journals, biographies, life histories, or narrative accounts of the curriculum, can probably be enhanced by a cross-disciplinary consideration of narrative, such as has been attempted here. If narrative is a research tool, the nature and function of the tool needs to be clearly established.

Narrative analysis could usefully be carried out at all levels of education, from the nursery or primary school to further and higher education, with both teachers and learners at all levels. This could be both a general inquiry into the nature of educational experience or a specifically focussed research project into such issues as participants' concepts of teaching and learning, curriculum issues, organization, evaluation, and the ever-important topic of teachers' and learners' thinking. The role of narrative and other schemas as influential or determining structures of expectations seems to be important in such areas and could profitably be investigated. It is also clearly possible to carry out narrative research in education on such topics as gender, race, social background and other areas of identity.

The use of narrative research and methods over the pre-service/in-service continuum of courses for teachers can also be developed, for example to investigate the important question of teacher change and professional development over stages of a career. Narrative research may reveal common patterns here, especially perhaps if focussed on specific issues, such as notions of discipline and control.

In the use of narratives for teacher training there is much to consider and develop, for example the differences between oral and written stories bears investigation, especially where oral and written stories, say from journals, are used in sequence so that there is an interweaving of the spoken and written narrative as it is composed and shared. The social dimension of this process, the interaction with experienced teachers and tutors, the effect of a group on a narrative, is probably an important variable: how does a story of the same event vary with different tellers, compared with many stories told by the same teacher?

A further key area for research is to explore the relationship between narrative and metaphor, both so common in teacher talk and both apparently so central in teacher thinking.

Conclusion

Since some scholars in every discipline in the social sciences are now engaged in narrative research and since each discipline has its own methods, a cross-disciplinary search for insight, implications and applications for narrative analysis in education can be long, perhaps unending. To conclude this book, a reminder of the importance of narratives for the teachers' world seems appropriate.

In narrative, teachers not only recall and report experience, they repeat it and recreate it. Through narrative, the meaning of experience is reorganized and reconstructed, both for tellers and audiences. In telling their narratives, teachers are rehearsing, redefining and regenerating their personal and professional selves, since self is what we believe ourselves to be, our self-narrative.

Teachers' narratives reflect their experiences. By encouraging the telling of their stories we encourage reflecting on experience, a refracting of it into significant parts so that it can be understood, the better to be remembered and shared. Positive stories shared between teachers provide direction, courage and hope in their work. Negative stories may be a social lubricant, reducing friction in schools and allowing them to function more smoothly. As teachers, or other professionals, the stories we tell tell us who we are and what we will become. Our stories are our professional world, the map of our experience.

Stories, in several senses, make sense. Given the personal, emotional, social, cognitive and cultural value in teachers' stories it is hardly surprising that they should be of interest to researchers. If, as White (1981) says, narratives translate knowing into telling then to carry out research through narrative analysis is to look at the telling to get back to the knowing. Teachers, too, as researchers, can analyze their own narratives to become, in Dewey's phrase (1938b) 'scholars of their own consciousness' (p. 123).

Teachers' narratives provide stories of their actual experiences — these we need to know about, for reasons theoretical and practical. Teachers' narratives tell us about their ways of seeing and thinking — these, also, we need to know about. Narrative analysis is one way to find out.

References

ABBOTT, V., BLACK, J.B. and SMITH, E.E. (1985) 'The representation of scripts in memory', *Journal of Memory and Language*, **24**, pp. 179–99.

ACKER, S. (1987) 'Primary school teaching as an occupation' in DELAMONT, S. (Ed.) *The Primary School Teacher*, London, Falmer Press, pp. 83–99.

AKINNASO, F.N. and AJIROTUTU, C.S. (1982) 'Performance and ethnic style in Job interviews' in GUMPERZ, J. (Ed.) *Language and Social Identity*, Cambridge, Cambridge University Press, pp. 119–44.

ATKINSON, P. (1990) *The Ethnographic Imagination: Textual Constructions of Reality*, London, Routledge.

BADDELEY, A.D. (1976) *The Psychology of Memory*, New York, Basic Books.

BAL, M. (1983) 'The narrating and the focalizing: A theory of the agents in narrative', *Style*, **17**, 2, pp. 234–69.

BAL, M. (1985) *Narratology: Introduction to the Theory of Narrative*, Toronto, University of Toronto Press.

BANFIELD, A. (1973) 'Narrative style and the grammar of direct and indirect speech', *Foundations of Language*, **10**, pp. 1–39.

BARCLAY, C.R. (1986) 'Schematization of autobiographical memory' in RUBIN, D.C. (Ed.) *Autobiographical Memory*, Cambridge, Cambridge University Press, pp. 82–99.

BARNLUND, D.C. (1975) *Private and Public Self in Japan and the United States*, Tokyo, Simul Press.

BARTHES, R. (1980) 'Introduction to the structural analysis of narrative' in PUGH, A.K., LEE, V.J. and SWANN, J. (Eds) *Language and Language Use*, London, Heinemann, pp. 244–273.

BARTLETT, F.C. (1932) *Remembering*, London, Cambridge University Press.

BASCOM, W. (1965) 'The forms of folklore: Prose narratives', *Journal of American Folklore*, **78**, pp. 3–20.

BASSO, K.H. (1984) ' "Stalking with stories": Names, places and moral narratives among the Western Apache' in BRUNER, E.M. (Ed.), *Text, Play and Story: The Construction and Reconstruction of Self and Society*, Washington D.C., American Ethnological Society, pp. 19–55.

BAUMAN, R. (1975) 'Verbal art as performance', *American Anthropologist*, 77, pp. 290–311.

BAUMAN, R. (1977) *Verbal Art as Performance*, Rowley, MA, Newbury House.

BAUMAN, R. (1986) *Story, Performance and Event*, Cambridge, Cambridge University Press.

BAUMAN, R. and SHERZER, J. (Eds) (1974) *Explorations in the Ethnography of Speaking*, Cambridge, Cambridge University Press.

DE BEAUGRANDE, R. (1982) 'The story of grammars and the grammars of stories', *Journal of Pragmatics*, 6, pp. 383–422.

DE BEAUGRANDE, R. and COLBY, B.N. (1979) 'Narrative models of interaction', *Cognitive Science*, 3, pp. 43–66.

DE BEAUGRANDE, R. (1980) *Text, Discourse and Process*, London, Longman.

DE BEAUGRANDE, R. and DRESSLER, W. (1981) *Introduction to Text Linguistics*, London, Longman.

BENNETT, G. (1983) ' "Rocky the Police Dog" and other tales: Traditional narrative in an occupational corpus', *Lore and Language*, 3, 8, pp. 1–19.

BERENDSEN, M. (1984) 'The teller and the observer: Narration and focalization in narrative texts', *Style*, 18, 2, pp. 40–58.

BERK, L. (1980) 'Education in lives: Biographic narrative in the study of educational outcomes', *Journal of Curriculum Theorizing*, 2, 2, pp. 88–154.

BERKMAN, S.C.J. (1978) 'She's writing antidotes: An examination of hospital employees' uses of stories about personal experiences', *Folklore Forum*, 11, pp. 48–54.

BERLAK, A. and H. (1981) *Dilemmas of Schooling, teaching and social change*, London, Methuen.

BLACK, J.R. (1984) 'Understanding and remembering stories' in ANDERSON, J.R. and KOSSLYN, S.M. (Eds) *Tutorials in Learning and Memory*, San Francisco, CA, Freeman, pp. 235–59.

BLACK, J.B. and WILENSKY, R. (1979) 'An evaluation of story grammars', *Cognitive Science*, 3, pp. 213–29.

BOOTH, W.C. (1987) *The rhetoric of Fiction*, 2nd ed., Harmondsworth, Penguin.

BOWER, G.H. (1976) 'Experiments in story understanding and recall', *Quarterly Journal of Experimental Psychology*, 28, pp. 511–34.

BOWER, G.H., BLACK, J.B. and TURNER, T.J. (1979) 'Scripts in memory for text', *Cognitive Psychology*, 11, pp. 177–220.

BOYD, E. and FALES, A. (1983) 'Reflective learning: Key to learning from experience', *Journal of Humanistic Psychology*, 23, 2, pp. 99–117.

BRANIGAN, E. (1992) *Narrative Comprehension and Film*, London, Routledge.

BREMOND, C. (1966) 'La Logique des Possibles Narratifs', *Communications*, 8, pp. 60–76.

BREMOND, C. (1973) *Logique du Récit*, Paris, Seuil.

BREWER, W.F. (1985) 'The story schema: Universal and culture-specific properties' in OLSEN, D.A., TORRANCE, N. and HILDYARD, A. (Eds) *Literacy, Language and Learning*, Cambridge, Cambridge University Press, pp. 167–94.

BREWER, F. (1986) 'What is autobiographical memory?' in RUBIN, D.C. (Ed.) *Autobiographical Memory*, Cambridge, Cambridge University Press, pp. 25–49.

BREWER, W.F. and LICHTENSTEIN, E.H. (1981) 'Event schemas, story schemas and story grammars' in LONG, J. and BADDELEY, A. (Eds) *Attention and Performance*, vol. xi, pp. 363–379. HILLSDALE, N.J, Lawrence Erlbaum.

BREWER, W.F. and LICHTENSTEIN, E.H. (1982) 'Stories are to entertain: A structural-affect theory of stories', *Journal of Pragmatics*, **6**, pp. 473–86.

BRIGGS, C.L. (1986) *Learning How to Ask: A Sociolinguistic Appraisal of the Role of the Interview in Social Science Research*. Cambridge, Cambridge University Press.

BRITTON, B.K. and PELLEGRINI, A.D. (Eds) (1990) *Narrative Thought and Narrative Language*, Hillsdale, NJ, Lawrence Erlbaum Associates.

BROWN, G. and YULE, G. (1983) *Discourse Analysis*, Cambridge, Cambridge University Press.

BROWN, R. and KULIK, J. (1982) 'Flashbulb memories' in NEISSER, U. (Ed.) *Memory Observed: Remembering in Natural Contexts*, San Francisco, CA, Freeman, pp. 23–40.

BROWN, R. L. Jr. and HERNDL, C.G. (1986) 'An ethnographic study of corporate writing: Job status as reflected in written text' in COUTURE, B. (Ed.) *Functional Approaches to Writing: Research Perspectives*, London, Francis Pinter.

BRUMBLE, H.D. (1990) *American Indian Autobiography*, Berkeley, CA, University of California Press.

BRUNER, J. (1986) *Actual Minds, Possible Worlds*, Cambridge, MA, Harvard University Press.

BRUNER, J. (1990) *Acts of Meaning*, Cambridge, MA, Harvard University Press.

BUCKHART, R. (1982) 'Eyewitness testimony' in NEISSER, U. (Ed.) *Memory Observed: Remembering in Natural Contexts*, San Francisco, Freeman, pp. 116–25.

BUTT, R.L., RAYMOND, D. and YAMAGISHI, L. (1988) 'Autobiographic praxis: Studying the formation of teachers' knowledge', *Journal of Curriculum Theorizing*, **7**, 4, pp. 87–164.

BUTT, R.L., RAYMOND, D., MCCUE, G. and YAMAGISHI, L. (1992) 'Collaborative autobiography and the teacher's voice' in GOODSON, I.F. (Ed.) *Studying Teachers' Lives*, London, Routledge.

BUTT, R.L. and RAYMOND, D. (1987) 'Arguments for using qualitative approaches in understanding teacher thinking: The case for biography', *Journal of Curriculum Theorizing*, **7**, 1, pp. 62–93.

BUTT, R.L. and RAYMOND, D. (1989) 'Studying the nature and development of teachers' knowledge using collaborative autobiography', *International Journal of Educational Research*, **13**, 4 pp. 403–19.

BUTT, R.L., TOWNSEND, D. and RAYMOND, D. (1990) 'Bringing reform to life: Teachers' stories and professional development', *Cambridge Journal of Education*, **20**, 3, pp. 255–68.

References

CALDERHEAD, J. (Ed.) (1987) *Exploring Teachers' Thinking*, London, Cassell.

CALDERHEAD, J. (Ed.) (1988) *Teachers' Professional Learning*, London, Falmer Press.

CARTER, R. and SIMPSON, P. (1982) 'The sociolinguistic analysis of narrative', *Belfast Working Papers in Linguistics*, 6, pp. 123–52.

CHAFE, W. (1990) 'Some things that narratives tell us about the mind' in BRITTON, B.K. and PELLEGRINI, A.D. (Eds) *Narrative Thought and narrative Language*, Hillsdale, NJ, Lawrence Erlbaum, pp. 79–98.

CHATMAN, S. (1978) *Story and Discourse: Narrative Structure in Fiction and Film*, Ithaca, NY, Cornell University Press.

CHATMAN, S. (1988) 'The representation of text types', *Textual Practice*, 2, pp. 22–9.

CLARK, B. (1983) 'The organizational saga in higher education' in BALDRIDGE, J.V. and DEAL, T. (Eds) *The Dynamics of Organizational Change in Education*, Berkeley, CA, McCutchan pp. 373–82.

CLEMENT, D. and COLBY, B.N. (1974) 'Folk narrative' in SEBEOK, T.A. (Ed.) *Current Trends in Linguistics*, vol. 12, The Hague, Mouton, pp. 809–33.

COFER, C.N. (1973) 'Constructive processes in memory', *American Scientist*, 60, pp. 537–43.

COHAN, S. and SHIRES, L.M. (1988) *Telling Stories: A Theoretical Analysis of Narrative Fiction*, New York, Routledge.

COLBY, B.N. (1966a) 'Cultural patterns in narrative', *Science*, 151, pp. 793–98.

COLBY, B.N. (1966b) 'The analysis of culture context and the patterning of narrative concern in texts', *American Anthropologist*, 68, pp. 374–88.

COLBY, B.N. (1973a) 'Analytical procedures in eidochronic study', *Journal of American Folklore*, 83, pp. 14–24.

COLBY, B.N. (1973b) 'A partial grammar of Eskimo folktales', *American Anthropologist*, 75, pp. 645–62.

COLBY, B.N. and PEACOCK, J.L. (1973) 'Narrative' in HONIGMENN, J.J. (Ed.) *Handbook of Social and Cultural Anthropology*, Chicago, IL, Rand McNally, pp. 613–36.

COLES, R. (1989) *The Call of Stories: Teaching and the Moral Imagination*. Boston, MA, Houghton Mifflin.

COLLINS, R. (1988) 'Theoretical continuities in Goffman's work' in DREW, P. and WOOTTON, A. (Eds) *Erving Goffman: Exploring the Interaction Order*, Oxford, Polity Press, pp. 41–63.

CONNELLY, F.M. and CLANDININ, D.J. (1987) 'On narrative method, biography and narrative unities in the study of teaching', *The Journal of Educational Thought*, 21, 3, pp. 130–9.

CONNELLY, F.M. and CLANDININ, D.J. (1988a) 'Narrative meaning: Focus on teacher education', *Elements* 19, 2, pp. 15–18.

CONNELLY, F.M. and CLANDININ, D.J. (1988b) *Teachers as Curriculum Planners: Narratives of Experience*, New York, Teachers' College Press.

CONNELLY, F.M. and CLANDININ, D.J. (1990) 'Stories of experience and narrative inquiry', *Educational Researcher*, 19, 5, pp. 2–14.

CONNELLY, F.M. and CLANDININ, J.M. (1986) 'On narrative method, personal philosophy, and narrative unities in the story of teaching', *Journal of Research in Science Teaching*, **23**, 4, pp. 293–310.

CORSARO, W.A. (1985) 'Sociological approaches to discourse analysis' in VAN DIJK, T.A. (Ed.) *Handbook of Discourse Analysis*, vol. 1, London, Academic Press, pp. 167–92.

CORTAZZI, M. (1989) 'Teachers' anecdotes: Access to cultural perspectives through narrative analysis unpublished PhD thesis, University of Leicester.

CORTAZZI, M. (1991) *Primary Teaching, How It Is — A Narrative Account*, London, David Fulton.

COULTHARD, M. (1977) *An Introduction to Discourse Analysis*, London, Longman.

CULLER, J. (1975) *Structuralist Poetics; Structuralism, Linguistics and the Study of Literature*, London, Routledge and Kegan Paul.

DALI, F. (1981) *Speech in Narrative*, Birmingham, English Language Research, University of Birmingham.

DEAL, T.E. (1985) 'The symbolism of effective schools'. *The Elementary School Journal*, **85**, 5, pp. 601–20.

DEAN, J.P. and WHYTE, W.F. (1975) 'How do you know if the informant is telling the truth?', *Human Organization*, **17**, pp. 34–36.

DEGH, L. (1985) ' "When I was six we moved West . . ." The theory of personal experience narrative', *New York Folklore*, **11**, 1–4, pp. 99–108.

DENSCOMBE, M. (1983) 'Interviews, accounts and ethnographic research on teachers' in HAMMERSLEY, M. (Ed.) *The Ethnography of Schooling*, Driffield, Nafferton.

DEWEY, J. (1910) *How We Think*, Lexington, MA, D.C. Heath.

DEWEY, J. (1938a) *Logic: The Theory of Inquiry*, New York, Holt, Rinehart and Winston.

DEWEY, J. (1938b) *Education and Experience*, New York, Collier Books.

DIAMOND, C.T.P. (1991) *Teacher Education as Transformation: A Psychological Perspective*, Milton Keynes, Open University Press.

VAN DIJK, T.A. (1975) 'Action, action description and narrative', *New Literary History*, **6**, pp. 274–94.

VAN DIJK, T.A. (1977a) 'Semantic macrostructures and knowledge frames in discourse comprehension' in JUST, M.A. and CARPENTER, P.A. (Eds), *Cognitive Processes in Discourse Comprehension*, New York, Wiley, pp. 3–32.

VAN DIJK, T.A. (1977b) *Text and Context: Explorations in the Semantics and Pragmatics of Discourse*, London, Longman.

VAN DIJK, T.A. (Ed.) (1980) 'Story comprehension', *Poetics*, no. 9.

VAN DIJK, T.A. (1984) *Prejudice in Discourse: An Analysis of Ethnic Prejudice in Cognition and Conversation*, Amsterdam, John Benjamins.

VAN DIJK, T.A. (1988a) *News Analysis*, Hillsdale, NJ, Lawrence Erlbaum.

VAN DIJK, T.A. (1988b) *News as Discourse*, Hillsdale, NJ, Lawrence Erlbaum.

DREW, P. and WOOTTON, A. (Eds) (1988) *Erving Goffman: Exploring the Interaction Order*, Oxford, Polity Press.

DOYLE, W. (1990) 'Classroom knowledge as a foundation for teaching', *Teachers' College Record*, **91**, 3, pp. 347–59.

EAGLETON, T. (1983) *Literary Theory: An Introduction*, Oxford, Blackwell.

EGAN, K. (1988) *Primary Understanding: Education in Early Childhood*, New York, Routledge.

EGAN, K. (1989) 'The scope of the science text: A function of stories' in DE CASTELL, S., LUKE, A., and LUKE, C. (Eds) *Language, Authority and Criticism*, London, Falmer Press.

ELBAZ, F. (1990) 'Knowledge and discourse: The evolution of research on teacher thinking' in DAY, C., POPE, M. and DENICOLO, P. (Eds) *Insights into Teacher Thinking and Practice*, London, Falmer Press.

FAWCETT, R.P., HALLIDAY, M.A.K., LAMB, S.M. and MAKKAI, A. (1984) *The Semiotics of Culture and Language*, vol. 2, London, Pinter.

FEIMAN-NEMSER, S. and FLODEN, R.E. (1985) 'The cultures of teaching' in WITTROCK, M.C. (Ed.) *Handbook of Research in Teaching*, New York, Macmillan pp. 505–25.

FORSTER, E.M. (1927) *Aspects of the Novel*, New York, Harcourt, Brace and World.

FREEMAN, L.C., ROMNEY, A.K. and FREEMAN, S.C. (1987) 'Cognitive structure and informant accuracy', *American Anthropologist*, **8**, pp. 310–25.

GARNHAM, A. (1983) 'What's wrong with story grammars?' *Cognition*, **15**, pp. 145–154.

GARNHAM, A. (1985) *Psycholinguistics, Central Topics*, London, Methuen.

GARNHAM, A. (1988) 'Understanding' in CLAXTON, G. (Ed.) *Growth Points in Cognition*, London, Routledge.

GARVIE, E. (1990) *Story as Vehicle*, Clevedon, Multilingual Matters.

GENETTE, G. (1980) *Narrative Discourse*, Oxford, Blackwell.

GERGEN, M. (1988) 'Narrative structures in social explanation' in ANTAKI, C. (Ed.) *Analysing Everyday Explanation, A Casebook of Methods*, London, Sage Publications.

GIBSON, T. (1973) *Teachers Talking: Aims, Methods, Attitudes to Change*, London, Allen Lane.

GLENN, C.G. (1978) 'The role of episodic structure of story length in children's recall of simple stories', *Journal of Verbal Learning and Verbal Behaviour*, **17**, pp. 229–47.

GOFFMAN, E. (1969) *The Presentation of Self in Everyday Life*, Harmondsworth, Penguin.

GOFFMAN, E. (1975) *Frame Analysis: An Essay on the Organization of Experience*, Harmondsworth, Penguin

GOFFMAN, E. (1981) *Forms of Talk*, Oxford, Blackwell.

GOMULICKI, B.R. (1956) 'Recall as an abstractive process', *Acta Psychologica*, **12**, pp. 77–94.

GOODWIN, C. (1984) 'Notes on story structure and the organization of participation' in ATKINSON, J.M. and HERITAGE, J. (Eds) *Structures of Social Action: Studies in Conversation Analysis*, Cambridge, Cambridge University Press, pp. 225–46.

GOODSON, I. (1991) 'Teachers' lives and educational research' in GOODSON, I.F. and WALKER, R. (Eds) *Biography, Identity and Schooling: Episodes in Educational Research*, London, Falmer Press.

GOODSON, I.F. (1992) 'Studying teachers' lives, an emergent field of inquiry' in GOODSON, I.F. (Ed.) *Studying Teachers' Lives*, London, Routledge, pp. 1–17.

GREIMAS, A.J. (1971) 'Narrative grammar: Units and levels', *Modern Language Notes*, **86**, 6, pp. 793–806.

GREIMAS, A. (1983) *Structural Semantics: An Attempt at a Method*, Lincoln, NB, University of Nebraska Press.

GREENE, J. (1986) *Language Understanding: A Cognitive Approach*, Milton Keynes, Open University Press.

GRIMES, J.E. (1975) *The Thread of Discourse*, The Hague, Mouton.

GRIMES, J.E. (1978) 'Narrative studies in oral texts' in DRESSLER, W.U. (Ed.) *Current Trends in Text Linguistics*, Berlin, de Gruyter, pp. 123–32.

GRIMES, J.E. (Ed.) (1978) *Papers on Discourse*, Dallas, TX, Institute of Linguistics.

GROSSE, E.U. (1978) 'French Structuralist views on narrative grammar' in DRESSLER, W.U. (Ed.) *Current Trends in Textlinguistics*, Berlin, de Gruyter, pp. 155–73.

GRUMET, M.R. (1980) 'Autobiography and reconceptualization', *Journal of Curriculum Theorizing*, **2**, 2, pp. 155–8.

GRUMET, M.R. (1981) 'Restitution and reconstruction of educational experience: An autobiographical method for curriculum theory' in LAWN, M. and BARTON, L. (Eds) *Rethinking Curriculum Studies: A Radical Approach*, London, Croom Helm, pp. 115–30.

GRUMET, M.R. (1990) 'Voice: The search for a feminist rhetoric for educational studies', *Cambridge Journal of Education*, **20**, 2, pp. 277–82.

GUDMUNDSDOTTIR, S. (1990) 'Curriculum stories: Four case studies of social studies teaching' in DAY, C., POPE, M. and DENICOLO, P. (Eds) *Insights into Teacher Training and Practice*, London, Falmer Press.

GUDMUNDSDOTTIR, S. (1991) 'Story-maker, story-teller: narrative structures in curriculum', *Journal of Curriculum Studies*, **23**, 3, pp. 207–18.

GUMPERZ, J. and HYMES, D. (Eds) (1972) *Directions in Sociolinguistics: The Ethnography of Communication*, New York, Holt, Rinehart and Winston.

HARDY, B. (1987) *The Collected Essays of Barbara Hardy*, vol. 1, Sussex, Harvester Press.

HASTRUP, K. (1992) 'Writing ethnography, state of the art' in OKELY, J. and CALLAWAY, H. (Eds) *Anthropology and Autobiography* London, Routledge, pp. 116–33.

HATCH, E. (1992) *Discourse and Language Education*, Cambridge, Cambridge University Press.

HAWKES, T. (1977) *Structuralism and Semiotics*, London, Methuen.

HEATH, S.B. (1983) *Ways with Words: Language, Life and Work in Communities and Classrooms*, Cambridge, Cambridge University Press.

HENDRICKS, W.O. (1973) *Essays on Semiolinguistics and Verbal Art*, The Hague, Mouton.

HESTER, H. (1983) *Stories in the Multilingual Primary Classroom*, London, ILEA.

HILSUM, S. (1972) *The Teacher as Work*, Slough, NFER.

HILSUM, S. and CANE, B.S. (1971) *The Teacher's Day*, Slough, NFER.

HOEY, M. (1983) *On the Surface of Discourse*, London, George Allen and Unwin.

HOEY, M. and WINTER, E. (1986) 'Clause relations and the writer's communicative task' in COUTUR, B. (Ed.) *Functional Approaches to Writing, Research Perspectives*, London, Francis Pinter, pp. 120–41.

HOLLY, M.L. (1989) 'Reflective writing and the spirit of inquiry', *Cambridge Journal of Education*, **19**, 1, pp. 71–80.

HSU, F. (1981) *Americans and Chinese, Passage to Differences*, Honolulu, University of Hawaii.

HUNTER, I.M.L. (1964) *Memory*, Harmondsworth, Penguin.

HYMES, D. (1974) 'Ways of Speaking' in BAUMAN, R. and SHERZER, J. (Eds) *Explorations in the Ethnography of Speaking*, Cambridge, Cambridge University Press, pp. 433–51.

HYMES, D. (1975) 'Breakthrough into performance' in BEN AMOS, D. and GOLDSTEIN, K.S. (Eds) *Folklore, Performance and Communication*, The Hague, Mouton, pp. 11–74.

HYMES, D. (1977) *Foundations in Sociolinguistics: An Ethnographic Approach*, London, Tavistock Publications.

JASON, H. and SEGAL, D. (Eds) (1977) *Patterns in Oral Literature*, The Hague, Mouton.

JEFFERSON, G. (1978) 'Sequential aspects of storytelling in conversation' in SCHENKEIN, J. (Ed.) *Studies in the Organization of Conversation*, New York, Academic Press, pp. 219–48.

JOHNSON, N.S. and MANDLER, J.M. (1980) 'A tale of two structures: Underlying and surface forms in stories, *Poetics*, **9**, pp. 52–86.

JOHNSON-LAIRD, P.N. (1983) *Mental Models*, Cambridge, Cambridge University Press.

JORDAN, M.P. (1984) *Rhetoric of Everyday English Texts*, London, George Allen and Unwin.

KALCIK, S. (1975) '"... like Ann's gynecologist or the time I was almost raped"', *Journal of American Folklore*, **88**, pp. 3–11.

KANT, I. (1787) *Critique of Pure Reason*, transl. N.K. SMITH (1968) London, Macmillan.

KEENAN, J.M., MACWHINNEY, B. and MAYHEW, D. (1982) 'Pragmatics in memory: A study of natural conversation' in NEISSER, U. (Ed.) *Memory Observed, Remembering in Natural Contexts*, San Francisco, CA, Freeman.

KENDON, A. (1988) 'Goffman's approach to face to face interaction' in DREW, P. and WOOTON, A. (Eds) *Erving Goffman, Exploring the Interaction Order*, Oxford, Polity Press, pp. 14–42.

KERNAN, K.T. (1977) 'Semantic and expressive elaboration in children's narratives' in ERVIN-TRIPP, S. (Ed.) *Child Discourse*, New York, Academic Press, pp. 91–102.

KINTSCH, W. (1974) *The Representation of Meaning in Memory*, HILLSDALE, NJ, Erlbaum-Wiley.

KINTSCH, W. (1976) 'Memory for prose' in COFER, C. (Ed.) *The Structure of Human Memory*, San Francisco, Freeman, pp. 90–113.

KINTSCH, W. (1977a) *Memory and Cognition*, New York, Wiley.

KINTSCH, W. (1977b) 'On comprehending stories' in JUST, M.A. and CARPENTER, P.A. (Eds) *Cognitive Processes in Comprehension*, New York, Wiley, pp. 33–62.

KINTSCH, W. (1985) 'Text processing: A psychological model' in VAN DIJK, T.A. (Ed.) *Handbook of Discourse Analysis*, vol. 2, London, Academic Press, pp. 231–43.

KINTSCH, W. and VAN DIJK, T.A. (1983) *Strategies of Discourse Comprehension*, London, Academic Press.

KINTSCH, W. and GREENE, E. (1978) 'The role of culture-specific schemata in the comprehension and recall of stories', *Discourse Processes*, 1, pp. 1–13.

KIRSHENBLATT-GIMBLETT, B. (1974) 'The concept and varieties of narrative performance in East European Jewish culture' in BAUMAN, R. and SHERZER, J. (Eds) *Explorations in the Ethnography of Speaking*, Cambridge, Cambridge University Press, pp. 283–308.

KIRSHENBLATT-GIMBLETT, B. (1975) 'A parable in context: A social interactional analysis of storytelling performance' in BEN AMOS, D. and GOLDSTEIN, K.S. (Eds) *Folklore, Performance and Communication*, The Hague, Mouton, pp. 105–14.

KNOWLES, J.G. and HOLT-REYNOLDS, D. (1991) 'Shaping pedagogies through personal histories in pre-service teacher education', *Teachers' College Record*, **93**, 1, pp. 87–113.

KNOWLES, J.G. (1992) 'Models for understanding pre-service and beginning teachers' biographies' in GOODSON, I.F. (Ed.) *Studying Teachers' Lives* London, Routledge.

KRESS, G. and FOWLER, R. (1983) 'Interviews' in FOWLER, R., HODGE, B., KRESS, G. and TREW, T. (Eds) *Language and Control*, London, Routledge and Kegan Paul, pp. 63–80.

LABOV, W. (1971) 'Methodology' in DINGWALL, W.O. (Ed.) *A Survey of Linguistic Science*, Maryland, University of Maryland, Linguistics Program, pp. 412–97.

LABOV, W. (1972) 'The transformation of experience in narrative syntax' in LABOV, W. (Ed.) *Language in the Inner City*, Philadelphia, PA, University of Pennsylvania, pp. 352–96.

LABOV, W. (1981) 'Speech actions and reactions in personal narrative, in *Georgetown University Round Table in Language and Linguistics*, pp. 219–47.

LABOV, W., COHEN, P., ROBINS, C. and LEWIS, J. (1968) *A Study of the Non-Standard English of Negro and Puerto-Rican Speakers in New York City*, vol. 2. Washington, D.C., Office of Education, U.S. Dept. of Health, Education and Welfare, pp. 286–333.

LABOV, W. and FANSHEL, D. (1977) *Therapeutic Discourse, Psychotherapy as Conversation*, New York, Academic Press.

LABOV, W. and WALETSKY, J. (1967) 'Narrative analysis: Oral versions of personal experience' in HELM, J. (Ed.) *Essays on the Verbal and Visual Arts*, Seattle, American Ethnological Society, pp. 12–44.

LEJEUNE, P. (1974) *Le Pacte Autobiographique*, Paris, Editions du Seuil.

LEVINSON, S. (1983) *Pragmatics*, Cambridge, Cambridge University Press.

LEVI-STRAUSS, C. (1968) *Structural Anthropology*, London, Allen Lane.

LICHTENSTEIN, E.H. and BREWER, W.F. (1980) 'Memory for goal-directed events', *Cognitive Psychology*, 12, pp. 412–45.

LONGACRE, R. (1976) *An Anatomy of Speech Notions*, Lisse, Peter de Ridder.

LONGACRE, R. and LEVINSOHN, S. (1978) 'Field analysis of discourse' in DRESSLER, W.U. (Ed.) *Current Trends in Text Linguistics*, Berlin, de Gruyter, pp. 103–22.

LORD, A.B. (1965) *The Singer of Tales*, New York, Atheneum.

LOUDEN, W. (1991) *Understanding Teaching, Continuity and Change in Teachers' Knowledge*, London, Cassell.

LYTLE, S.L. and COCHRAN-SMITH, M. (1990) 'Learning from teacher research: A working typology', *Teachers' College Record*, 22, 1, pp. 83–103.

MASS, J. (1991) 'Writing and reflection in teacher education' in TABACHNIK, B.R. and ZEICHNER, K.M. (Eds) *Issues and Practices in Inquiry Oriented Teacher Education*, London, Falmer Press, pp. 211–25.

MACLEAN, M. (1988) *Narrative as Performance: A Beaudelairean Experiment*, London, Routledge.

MCCARTHY, M. (1991) *Discourse Analysis for Language Teachers*, Cambridge, Cambridge University Press.

MANDLER, J.M. (1978) 'A code in the node: The use of a story schema in retrieval', *Discourse Processes*, 1, pp. 14–35.

MANDLER, J.M. (1982) 'Another story of grammars, comments on Beaugrande's "The Story of Grammars and the Grammars of Stories"', *Journal of Personality and Social Psychology*, 35, pp. 63–78.

MANDLER, J.M. and JOHNSON, N.S. (1977) 'Remembrance of things parsed: Story structure and recall', *Cognitive Psychology*, 9, 1, pp. 11–151.

MANDLER, J., SCRIBNER, S., COLE, M. and DEFOREST, M. (1980) 'Cross-cultural invariance in story recall', *Child development*, 51, pp. 19–26.

MARCUS, H. (1977) 'Self schemata and processing information about the self', *Journal of Personality and Social Psychology*, 35, pp. 63–78.

MARSHALL, N. (1984) 'Discourse analysis as a guide for informal assessment of comprehension' in FLOOD, J.F. (Ed.) *Promoting Reading Comprehension*, Newark, Delaware, International Reading Association.

MARTIN, W. (1986) *Recent Theories of Narrative*, Ithaca, NY, Cornell University Press.

MEAD, G.H. (1934) *Mind, Self and Society*, Chicago, IL, Chicago University Press.

MEYER, B.J.F. (1975) *The Organization of Prose and its Effects on Memory*, Amsterdam, North Holland.

MINSKY, M. (1975) 'A framework for representing knowledge' in WINSTON, P. (Ed.) *The Psychology of Computer Vision*, New York, McGraw-Hill.

MISHLER, E.G. (1986) *Research Interviewing: Context and Narrative*, Cambridge, MA, Harvard University Press

MITCHELL, W.J.T. (Ed.) (1981) *On Narrative*, Chicago, IL, Chicago University Press.

MITROFF, I.I. and KILMANN, R.H. (1975) 'Stories managers tell: A new tool for organizational problem solving', *Management Review*, **64**, pp. 18–28.

MOERMAN, M. (1973) 'The use of precedent in natural conversation: A study in practical reasoning', *Semiotica*, **9**, pp. 193–210.

NIAS, J. (1989) *Primary Teachers Talking, a study of teaching as work*, London, Routledge.

NEISSER, U. (1982) *Memory Observed, Remembering in Natural Contexts*, San Francisco, CA, Freeman.

OKELY, J. (1992) 'Anthropology and autobiography' in OKELY, J. and CALLAWAY, H. (Eds) *Anthropology and Autobiography*, London, Routledge.

OLNEY, J. (1972) *Metaphors of Self: The Meaning of Autobiography*, Princeton, NJ, Princeton University Press.

ONG, W. (1982) *Orality and Literacy: The Technologizing of the Word*, London, Methuen.

PETERSON, C. and MCCABE, A. (1983) *Developmental Psycholinguistics: Three Ways of looking at a Child's Narrative*, New York, Plenum Press.

PINAR, W.F. (1988) 'Autobiography and the architecture of self', *Journal of Curriculum Theorizing*, **8**, 1, pp. 7–35.

PINAR, W.F. and GRUMET, M.R. (1976) *Toward a Poor Curriculum*, Dubuque, Iowa, Kendall/Hunt.

PLATT, M.L. (1977) *Towards a Speech Act Theory of Literary Analysis*, Bloomington, IN, Indiana University Press.

POLANYI, L. (1979) 'So what's the point?' *Semiotica*, **25**, 3/4, pp. 207–41.

POLANYI, L. (1982a) 'The Nature of Meaning in Stories in Conversation', *Studies in Twentieth Century Literature*, **6**, 1, pp. 51–65.

POLANYI, L. (1982b) 'Linguistic and Social Constraints on Storytelling', *Journal of Pragmatics*, **6**, pp. 509–524.

POLANYI, L. (1984) 'Literary complexity in everyday storytelling' in TANNEN, D. (Ed.) *Spoken and Written Language*, Norwood, NJ, Ablex.

POLANYI, L. (1985) *Telling the American Story: A structural and Cultural Analysis of Conversational Storytelling*, Norwood, NJ, Ablex.

POLLARD, A. (1985) *The Social World of the Primary School*, London, Cassell.

POLLARD, A. and TANN, S. (1987) *Reflective Teaching in the Primary School*, London, Cassell.

POLKINGHORNE, D.E. (1988) *Narrative Knowing and the Human Sciences*, Albany, NY, State University of New York Press.

POWELL, R.R. (1992) 'The influence of prior experiences on pedagogic constructs of traditional and non-traditional pre-service teachers', *Teaching and Teacher Education*, **8**, 3, pp. 225–38.

PRESTON, R.J. (1978) *Cree Narrative: Expressing the Personal Meanings of Events*, Ottawa, National Museum of Man, Canadian Ethnology Service.

PRINCE, G. (1973) *A Grammar of Stories*, The Hague, Mouton.

PRINCE, G. (1982) *Narratology: the Form and Function of Narrative*, The Hague, Mouton.

PROPP, V.J. (1968/1928) *Morphology of the Folktale*, Austin, TX, University of Texas Press.

RICHERT, A.E. (1991) 'Case methods and teacher education: Using cases to teach teacher reflection' in TABACHNIK, B.R. and ZEICHNER K.M. (Eds) *Issues and Practices in Inquiry Oriented Teacher Education*, London, Falmer Press, pp. 130–50.

RICOEUR, P. (1981) 'Narrative time' in MITCHELL, W.J.T. (Ed.) *On Narrative*, London, University of Chicago Press, pp. 165–86.

RICOEUR, P. (1984) *Time and Narrative*, vols. 1, 2. Chicago, IL, University of Chicago Press.

RIMMON-KENAN, S. (1983) *Narrative Fiction: Contemporary Poetics*, London, Methuen.

ROSEN, B. (1988) *And None of it was Nonsense: The Power of Storytelling in School*, London, Mary Glasgow Publications.

ROSEN, B. (1991) *Shapers and Polishers: Teachers as Storytellers*, London, Mary Glasgow Publications.

RUMELHART, D.E. (1975) 'Notes on a schema for stories' in BOBROW, D.G. and COLLINS, A. (Eds) *Representation and Understanding: Studies in Cognitive Science*, London, Academic Press, pp. 211–36.

RUMELHART, D.E. (1977) 'Understanding and summarizing brief stories' in LABERGE, D. and SAMUELS, S.J. (Eds) *Basic Processes in Reading: perception and Comprehension*, New York, Wiley, pp. 265–303.

RYAVE, A. (1978) 'On the achievement of a series of stories' in SCHENKEIN, J. (Ed.) *Studies in the Organization of Conversational Interaction*, New York, Academic Press, pp. 113–32.

SACKS, H. (1972) 'On the analysability of stories by children' in GUMPERZ, J. and HYMES, D. (Eds) *Directions in Sociolinguistics*, New York, Holt, Rinehart and Winston, pp. 325–45.

SACKS, H. (1973) 'On some puns: With some intimations' in SHUY, R. (Ed.) *Sociolinguistics: Current Trends and Perspectives*, Washington, DC, Georgetown University Press, pp. 135–44.

SACKS, H. (1974) 'An analysis of the course of a joke's telling in conversation' in BAUMAN, R. and SCHERZER, J. (Eds) *Explorations in the Ethnography of Speaking*, Cambridge, Cambridge University Press, pp. 337–53.

SACKS, H., SCHEGLOFF, E. and JEFFERSON, G. (1974) 'A simplest systematics for the organization of turn-taking in conversation', *Language*, 50, pp. 696–735.

SACKS, H. (1984) 'On doing "being ordinary" in ATKINSON, J.M. and HERITAGE, J. (Eds) *Structures of Social Action, Studies in Conversation Analysis*, Cambridge, Cambridge University Press.

SARBIN, T.R. (Ed.) (1986) *Narrative Psychology: The Storied Nature of Human Conduct*, New York, Praeger.

SANTINO, J. (1978a) 'Characteristics of occupational narratives' *Western Folklore*, **34**, pp. 199–212.

SANTINO, J. (1978b) 'Flew the ocean in a plane: An investigation of airline occupational narrative', *Journal of the Folklore Institute*, **15**, pp. 189–208.

SAVILLE-TROIKE, M. (1982) *The Ethnography of Communication*, Oxford, Blackwell.

SCHANK, R.C. (1975) 'The structure of episodes in memory' in BOBROW, D.G. and COLLINS, A. (Eds) *Representation and Understanding: Studies in Cognitive Science*, London, Academic Press.

SCHANK, R. (1976) 'The role of memory in language processing' in COFER, C.N. (Ed.) *The Structure of Human Memory*, San Francisco, CA, Freeman.

SCHEGLOFF, E. (1972) 'Sequencing in conversational openings' in GUMPERZ, J. and HYMES, D. (Eds) *Directions in Sociolinguistics*, New York, Holt, Rinehart and Winston, pp. 346–80.

SCHEGLOFF, E. (1978) 'On some questions and ambiguities in conversation' in DRESSLER, W.V. (Ed.) *Current Trends in Text Linguistics*, Berlin, Walter de Gruyter, pp. 80–101.

SCHEGLOFF, E. (1988) 'Goffman and the analysis of conversation' in DREW, P. and WOOTTON, A. (Eds) *Erving Goffman: Exploring the Interaction Order*, Cambridge, Polity Press, pp. 89–135.

SCHEUB, H. (1975) 'Oral narrative process and the use of models', *New Literary History*, **6**, 2, pp. 353–77.

SCHIFFRIN, D. (1988) 'Conversation analysis' in NEWMEYER, F. (Ed.) *Language: The Sociocultural Context*, Cambridge, Cambridge University Press, pp. 251–76.

SCHLEIFER, R. (1987) *A.J. Greimas and the Nature of Meaning: Linguistics, Semiotics and Discourse Theory*, London, Croom Helm.

SCHOLES, R. and KELLOGG, R. (1966) *The Nature of Narrative*, New York, Oxford University Press.

SCHON, D. (1983) *The Reflective Practitioner*, New York, Basic Books.

SCHON, D. (1987) *Educating the Practitioner*, San Francisco, CA, Jossey-Bass.

SCHWAB, J. (1971) 'The practical arts of eclectic', *School Review*, August, pp. 493–543.

SCOLLON, R. and SCOLLON, S. (1981) *Narrative, Literacy and Face in Interethnic Communication*, Norwood, NJ, Ablex.

SCOLLON, R. and SCOLLON, S. (1984) 'Cooking it up and boiling it down: Abstracts in Athabascan children's story retellings' in TANNEN, D. (Ed.) *Coherence in Spoken Discourse*, Norwood, NJ, Ablex, pp. 173–97.

SELDEN, R. (1985) *A Reader's Guide to Contemporary Literary Theory*, Brighton, Harvester Press.

SERGIOVANNI, T.J. (1985) 'Understanding reflective practice', *Journal of Curriculum and Supervision*, **1**, 4, pp. 353–59.

SHEPPHERD, J. (1988) *A Leaf of Honey and Proverbs of the Rainforest*, London, Baha'i Publishing Trust.

SHERZER, J. (1987) 'A discourse-centred approach to language and culture', *American Anthropologist*, **89**, pp. 295–309.

SILVERMAN, D. (1973) 'Interview talk: Bringing off a research instrument', *Sociology*, 7, 1, pp. 31–48.

STEIN, N.L. and GLENN, C.G. (1979) 'An analysis of story comprehension in elementary school children' in FREEDLE, R.O. (Ed.) *New Directions in Discourse Processing*, Norwood, NJ, Ablex, pp. 53–120.

STEIN, N. and NEZWORSKI, T. (1978) 'The effects of organization and instructional set on story memory', *Discourse Processes*, **1**, pp. 177–194.

STEIN, N. (1982) 'The definition of a story', *Journal of Pragmatics*, **6**, pp. 487–504.

STUBBS, M. (1983) *Discourse Analysis: The Sociolinguistic Analysis of Natural Language*, Oxford, Blackwell.

TABACHNIK, B.R. and ZEICHNER, K. (Eds) (1991) *Issues and Practices in Inquiry Oriented Teacher Education*, London, Falmer Press.

TANNEN, D. (1979) 'What's in a frame? Surface evidence for underlying expectations' in FREEDLE, R.O. (Ed.) *New Directions in Discourse Processing*, Norwood, NJ, Ablex. pp. 137–81.

TANNEN, D. (1980) 'A comparative analysis of oral narrative strategies: Athenian Greek and American English' in CHAFE, W.L. (Ed.) *The Pear Stories: Cognitive, Cultural and Linguistic Aspects of Narrative Production*, Norwood, NJ, Ablex, pp. 51–87.

TARPY, R.M. and MAYER, R.E. (1978) *Foundations of Learning and Memory*, Glenview, IL, Scott Foresman.

TAYLOR, G. (1986) 'The development of style in children's fictional narrative' in WILKINSON, A. (Ed.) *The Writing of Writing*, Milton Keynes, Open University Press, pp. 215–33.

TAYLOR, T. and CAMERON, D. (1987) *Analysing Conversation: Rules and Units of the Structure of Talk*, Oxford, Pergamon.

THORNDYKE, P.W. (1977) 'Cognitive structures in comprehension and memory of narrative discourse', *Cognitive Psychology*, **9**, 1, pp. 77–110.

THORNDYKE, P. (1984) 'Applications of schema theory in cognitive research' in ANDERSON, J.R. and KOSSLYN, S.M. (Eds) *Tutorials in Learning and Memory: Essays in Honour of Gordon Bower*, San Francisco, CA, Freeman, pp. 167–92.

THORNDYKE, P.W. and YEKOVICH, F.A. (1980) 'A critique of schema-based theories of human story memory', *Poetics*, **9**, pp. 23–49.

TODOROV, T. (1969) *Grammaire du Décameron*, The Hague, Mouton.

TODOROV, T. (1969) 'Structural analysis of narrative, *Novel*, **3**, pp. 70–6.

TODOROV, T. (1977) *The Poetics of Prose*, Oxford, Blackwell.

TOELKEN, J.B. (1969) 'The "Pretty Language" of Yellowman: Genre, mode and texture in Navajo Coyote Narratives', *Genre*, **2**, 3, pp. 211–35.

TOELKEN, J.B. (1975) 'Folklore, worldview and communication' in BEN AMOS,

D. and GOLDSTEIN, K.S. (Eds) *Folklore, Performance and Communication*, The Hague, Mouton, pp. 265–86.

TOOLAN, M.J. (1988) *Narrative: A Critical Linguistic Introduction*, London, Routledge.

TSITSIPIS, L.D. (1983) 'Narrative performance in a dying language: Evidence from Albanian in Greece', *Word*, **34**, 1, pp. 25–36.

WALKER, R. (1985) *Doing Research: A Handbook for Teachers*, London, Methuen.

WATSON, K.A. (1972) *The rhetoric of narrative structure: A sociolinguistic analysis of stories told by part-Hawaiian children*, PhD thesis, University of Hawaii.

WEINTRAUB, K. (1978) *The Value of the Individual: Self and Circumstance in Autobiography*, Chicago, IL, Chicago University Press.

WHITE, H. (1981) 'The value of narrativity' in MITCHELL, W.J.T (Ed.) *On Narrative*, London University of Chicago Press, pp. 1–25.

WHITE, J.J. (1991) 'War stories: Invitations to reflect on practice' in TABACHNIK, B.R. and ZEICHNER K.M. (Eds) *Issues and Practices in Inquiry Oriented Teacher Education*, London, Falmer Press, pp. 226–52.

WILKINSON, J. (1986) 'Describing children's writing: Text evaluation and teaching strategies' in HARRIS, J. and WILKINSON, J. (Eds) *Reading Children's Writing: A Linguistic View*, London, George Allen and Unwin, pp. 11–31.

WOLFSON, N. (1976) 'Speech events and natural speech: Some implications for sociolinguistic methodology', *Language in Society*, **5**, pp. 189–209.

WOLFSON, N. (1982) *The Conversational Historical Present in American English Narrative*, Dordrecht, Foris.

WOOD, D.R. (1992) 'Teaching narratives: A source of faculty development and evaluation', *Harvard Educational Review*, **62**, 4, pp. 535–550.

WOODS, P. (1985) 'Conversations with teachers: Some aspects of life history methods', *British Educational Research Journal*, **11**, 1, pp. 13–26.

WOODS, P. (1990) *Teacher Skills and Strategies*, London, Falmer Press.

YEKOVICH, F.R. and THORNDYKE, P.W. (1981) 'An evaluation of alternative functional models of narrative schemata', *Journal of Verbal Learning and Verbal Behaviour*, **20**, pp. 454–69.

ZEICHNER, K.M. and LISTON, D.P. (1987) 'Teaching student teachers to reflect', *Harvard Educational Review*, **57**, 1, pp. 23–48.

ZEICHNER, K.M., TABACHNICK, R.B. and DENSMORE, K. (1987) 'Individual, institutional and cultural influences on the development of teachers' craft knowledge' in CALDERHEAD, J. (Ed.) *Exploring Teachers' Thinking*, London, Cassell, pp. 21–59.

ZHANG, X. and SANG, Y. (1986) *Chinese Profiles*, Beijing, Panda.

Index